Sonny Terry's
Country Blues Harmonica

Sonny Terry's
Country Blues Harmonica

by Sonny Terry
as told to Kent Cooper

Harp Instruction and Musical Transcriptions
by Fred "Boy Blue" Palmer

Oak Publications
New York • London • Tokyo • Sydney • Cologne

Acknowledgements/Fred Palmer:
I am grateful to all the people who helped. I would
particularly like to thank Bob Shatkin, whose kind
recommendation made it possible for me to be a part of
this book. Bob Wiley, John Mooney, Sharon Levia, Barbara
Wiley and George Sherman for their help and encouragement.
Special appreciation to Roger McCall and Bernie Kinball
of WCMF-FM in Rochester, N.Y. for their help in preparing
the record insert. Many thanks to Arthur Steinman and
Jason Shulman at Oak Publications for putting it all
together. And lastly, my deepest respect for Sonny Terry
and his influence on my life and feeling.

Photo Credits

Bill Boyarsky 19 top and bottom.
Courtesy of Kent Cooper 27, 32 top, 33.
David Gahr Front cover (courtesy of the Metropolitan
Museum of Art), 6, 32 bottom, 39, 40, 42, 66, 103,,109.
Courtesy of Brownie McGhee 77.
Courtesy of Emma Terry 12, 36, 93, Back cover.

Cover—Possibly the most well-known portrait of Sonny,
this photograph is in the collection of the Metropolitan
Museum of Art.

Back cover—An early publicity photo for Capitol Records,
probably taken in the late 1940's.

Music calligraphy by Marie Savettiere

Book design by Iris Weinstein

Distributed throughout the world by Music Sales Corporation:

33 West 60th Street, New York 10023
78 Newman Street, London W1P 3LA
4-26-22 Jingumae, Shibuya-ku, Tokyo 150
27 Clarendon Street, Artarmon, Sydney NSW 2064
Kölner Strasse 199, D-5000, Cologne 90

Contents

In them days I just as soon died—
except for my harmonica. It was like a friend who
didn't give a damn if I could see or not.

1911 - 1929

I was born in Greensboro, Georgia, in 1911. Borned in a tenant house on an old farm. Back in them days they had a mid-wife come around and your mama just yelled until it was over. Mama had us all in the same way.

From the time I remember, there were eight kids. That's not countin' the one what died a baby. The youngest of us was Jaboo, then come myself, then Willie, then Mitchell and Lou Daisy and Randel. I had a married sister, Roberta, who lived away from home, and an older brother over in Griffin, Georgia, name Reynolds.

Those years right in there was the only ones I ever had the feeling of a family. The kids at home got along pretty good. It was fun at the supper table, sitting around together with Mama serving, and everybody passing the food along. Everybody be talking at once, anxious to tell what they done that day. It seemed like it was the only real chance you had to talk to your parents, being they mostly worked all the time. If something was to worry your mind, there was always somebody big to tell it to.

After supper Paw sometimes took the harp down and played some numbers and Lou Daisy might make Mitchell dance with her. Mama even danced sometimes with one of us boys though mostly she was the serious kind.

We slept how most poor kids do, piled up in a couple old hard mattress beds. Times was tough back then, but we never went any too hungry. My father only worked on the farm, but he still owned his own chickens and a few cows and he killed seven or eight hogs every fall for the meat. There weren't all that much money about, but you didn't have to buy no more'n a little sugar and flour. Our clothes wasn't that good, but they hung to us all right.

Christmas time's when you mostly know you're poor. We didn't get so much, but it was fun. The whole day was spent going around to visit various folks. The older people would play music and sip whiskey while the kids fooled around. We didn't have no Christmas tree but hell, the woods was full of trees.

To me, my father was the most wonderful man in the world. I thought more of him than I did my mother. He'd get up any time of night we say we wanted something to eat and fix it. He done everything for us he could and he wasn't never mean about it. I had a heap of friends who couldn't say that. Old hard life had twisted and hurt their papas so bad you couldn't hardly be around them. I don't know, it might have been music that kept Daddy even-minded, just like it helped do for me later ... thru a lot of things ....

Mama never did care for what people said. She used to say "Nothing hurts me but a whipping."

She had a pretty good mean temper. But my father was easy until once't you got him mad, then nothing couldn't stop him. They told about the time when he was a young man and this fellow up and hit him with a stick. My father went to get his pistol but the fellow got away. He come around a few days later and say he wanted to make it up. He told my father, "Reuben, it was just I got so mad and down around the house, I had to take the fight out on somebody." My father told him, "You don't have to hit me for somebody else!"

My father worked hard, but he liked to have his fun, too. He used to play harmonica at them Saturday night fish fries and some such things. He didn't never do no blues. I never heard no blues before I was about eighteen years old. He done buckdances, reels and jigs, stuff as that that you can dance to. He could play the harp without using no hands, slide it along on his lips. I remember seeing a fellow back then called John Map could do the same thing.

Daddy used to keep his harmonica way up on the mantle piece when he wasn't using it. He go off to work, I'd push a chair over and get up and get it. Play my head off all day. I don't know, I just liked the sound of it. So, you know how it is when you care about something real bad, you can tell when it's been fooled with. One day Daddy asked me if I wasn't bothering his harmonica. I told him yeah.

He said, "Can you play it?"

Mama was right there. All the time she had heard me playing but she never said nothing to Daddy about it. But she spoke up then.

"Yeah, he can even play a tune."

"Let's hear it," Daddy said.

So I played off something for him. I don't remember the song, some old tune I'd heard him doing. When I got done, he laughed. "Well, tomorrow we got to get into town and get you a harp of your own," he said. "I think maybe you gonna do something with it."

Daddy was a great hunter. He hunted opossum, rabbits and even foxes. That's where I got the song the *Fox Chase*, listening to them dogs of his and the foxes going at it off in the woods. You don't never forget nothing like that.

Mama was a small lady, more light-skinned than my father. (He was real black like me.) Mama didn't give him no trouble about jealousy or nothing. Only just the way women gets evil sometimes—pushing at him.

A lot of my father's ways pushed back on her. My daddy could drink that liquor now. I remember one night when he played up on the river at some barbecue they had. The white folks give him a gallon jug of corn liquor. He must have played and drank his tail off that evening. So we had an old mule he'd driven up there. All a person had to do was get in the wagon and start the mule going and he'd bring you on home. That's 'cause the mule didn't know nothing else to do.

But that night, beings my father was laid out drunk, the mule decided to take a short cut on the way home. He followed across this footpath and got the wagon hung up on a narrow fence opening not too far from our house. The mule just bent his head down and went to eating.

I woke up and heard my father laying out there grunting and carrying on. I went to the door in my sleeping clothes.

My mother come awake herself and said, "Son, why don't you get some sleep?"

I said, "Naw, I can hear Paw out here. He out here in the gully somewhere."

She said, "No, he ain't."

I said, "Yeah, he is, too."

She went to get something to put on. I scrambled over there and jumped the fence and seen the mule. I got it backed out and we met my mother coming down the road. When my father seen her, he jumped out and started beating the mule with a shovel. "You know better'n to go that way!" he told the mule.

Mama say, "You devil you, quit hitting that mule! Don't hit him no more! You drunken rascal!"

My daddy didn't say nothing. He wouldn't cuss her.

That big jug of corn liquor was still there in the wagon. So when my father went stumbling inside, my mother asked me, "What's in that jar?"

I told her it was liquor. She said, "Well, you hide it where he won't find it tonight."

I carried it to the barn, but before I put it away, I took me a couple big ones. I liked to not got back in the house. It was good-tasting stuff, I'll tell you that. Made me hear ringing all over my head.

When Daddy got up in the morning, he'd forgot about the liquor. I told him, "Paw, I kept something for you." Then I went and brung him the jug.

He give me a big grin. "Where'd you get that, son?" he asked.

I told him it was in the wagon and he said, "Well, the Lord bless you, 'cause I thought I'd busted it."

Farmers live by the weather. My father was always worrying about the sun and rain, even if it wasn't his crops. That always made me aware of what each day was like, and it's still that way now. If it don't rain every so often, even in a city, I get bothered by it.

There wasn't too much trouble about black and whites down there then, 'cause wasn't nobody trying to do nothing. But still, you could feel it. As a small kid I knew whites treated us different and apart from everybody else. And I had sense enough to know that they didn't want no colored man going with no white woman. Everybody there's just raised that way, with the feeling that the white man is more than the colored. My father used to tell me not to worry about what other folks thought of me. He kept telling me that someday I'd realize I was as good as everybody—but I'd probably be away from there.

My people all belonged to the Baptist church. I believed in the church 'cause I was teached that, but I never did get religion too big. I seen these folks shouting and carrying on and I figured they must knowed something. They acted like they did, leastways. I'd kneel at the mourning bench with the rest of them, but I didn't never get no great feeling. I always believed there was a Lord or something, 'cause I know no human being couldn't make

9

the sun to shine and make it rain and thunder and go on like that.

I believe there's a God but I don't believe God's gonna come down here and put no food on your plate or put no money in your pocket. The Lord say he gonna help those who help themselves. I don't feel you got to go to church to make heaven. I think you can serve the Lord as good in your own way.

Even though I took up playing a harmonica when I was eight years old, I never did nothing any too serious with it 'till I hurt my eyes. I lost sight of my left eye when I was eleven years old. I had a little piece of stick I was hitting on the kitchen table and part of it flew into my eye. My father carried me to a doctor there in Greensboro, but they couldn't do nothing for me. The eye was just no good. I still kept going to school with the one eye I had, though.

I was old enough then to help in the work. I drove them tractor engines you turn land with and helped pick cotton in the fields. The fellow my father worked for, George Woods, was crazy about me. I used to cut wood for him and bring the cows in, helping him out. And he used to love to hear me play at the harmonica.

One of his cars was an old T-model that wasn't so good. He'd tell me, "Take it, Sonny. Go anywhere you want. If you tear it up, you have to walk back."

Off I'd go, zipping down them country roads and fill the thing up with pretty little girls. I loved to drive, get hurrying along and feel the wind blowing in the windows. I reckon I missed that as much as anything when I lost the last of my sight.

That happened when I was sixteen. I was playing with a little boy about four years old and he throwed a tiny piece of iron at me. It wasn't no longer than my finger but when it hit my good eye, I seen ninety eleven stars.

My father carried me to Atlanta, but it was too late, they couldn't do no good. The onliest thing I could see was the difference between night and day, the changes in the light. If somebody was wearing white, I could kind of make out a blurred shape where they were but that was all. I couldn't tell how good no woman looked.

In those days, I wouldn't go out of the house because I was ashamed. I just stayed back in my room, hearing my brothers and sisters playing and carrying on with neighbor kids. I'd hardly come to the supper table. I didn't think nobody wanted to fool with me and have to help me and all. 'Course then they didn't have no kinds of schools for the blind—not the poor blind anyway. The only thing I had any interest in was playing my harmonica and I kept on it night and day. I stayed hid, I reckon, for about two years.

My father moved us to Shelby, North Carolina. I believe he hoped he could do a little better for hisself up there. He went to work for the same man as my older brother Randel.

When we got there, neighborhood kids gathered 'round how they do when new folks move in. I held back while they carried the furniture indoors. I didn't want none of them to see me and laugh. In them days I just as soon died—except for my harmonica. It was like a friend who didn't give a damn if I could see or not.

But one day my mother waited until the other kids got gone, then she come into my room. She said, "Son, why don't you go out and play with them other children?"

I said, "They don't want to be playing with me out there, liable to be running over me and things 'cause I can't see good."

She said, "You just as good as anybody. . . . There's lots out there wish they was in as good a shape as you—ain't got no arms or legs, walking on their knees. There ain't no need to be staying in here, feeling sorry for yourself. You just as well get out there amongst the people, and be with them."

I started thinking, "Damn, that ain't helping me see. Not staying in here." When I thought that, it look like something just let loose inside me. I went out that same Saturday with my brother Willie and we got us a pint of liquor and got as drunk as we wanted to be . We come stumbling in the house late that night and my mama said to me, "Lord, here come another Reuben. Just like his father."

I didn't stay in no more after that. I went to dances and around just like anybody. I was almost my full-grown size by then.

I'll never forget the night a whole bunch of us boys were coming home from one of them country shindigs. We were walking along the highway 'bout eleven o'clock. I could make out carlights when they come rushing to us—Zoom! Zoom! Them whites was taking wild cuts at us and the others were helping pull me out of the way.

Finally, one of the fellows, Jim Moon, said, "Sonny, get ready to run—just catch hold of someone, 'cause the next one do it, I'm gonna bust the windshield in his face."

Jim could throw like a mule kick. He found him a good stone and waited. Then here come a car. We could hear them yelling out the side window, "Let's get us one, let's get us one!"

Jim Moon bust that glass—POW!—like a forty-five gun. The fellow was going so fast he couldn't get stopped right away. I heard him yelling from up the road, "Goddamn, I'm going back and shoot me one of them niggers!"

Everybody took off so fast I couldn't grab hold of none of them. I just followed hard after the rattle of their feet. They shot over a log fallen over this deep ditch, near-about as deep as a house, full of water. I run over it, too. It must have been fear holding me up, 'cause I didn't miss a step.

When we reached the other side, everyone jumped down in another ditch. I did too, and landed square on somebody's head.

"Get off my head, Sonny!" Jim Moon told me.

I slid to the other side of him and lay still. We could hear this white guy out there looking around. "I just want me one nigger," he said. Then he throwed his little gun in the air and fired it twice. I thought to myself, "He still don't know where we are or he'd shot somebody."

He finally got tired of searching and clumb back in the car. We heard him drive off and we jumped up, laughing and kidding about what we'd done. Them boys looked the log over and decided if I'd fell off, I'd drowned sure as shit.

When I got in that night, I realized I'd lost a new pair of glasses my father had got me the day before. My father come down with me the next morning to find them.

He killed hisself laughing when I told him what happened. He said, "I don't know what's gonna come of you, Sonny. You should have been home in bed and you out here running with them other boys."

He couldn't believe it when I showed him the log. Daddy tossed a stone into the water and said, "You'd never have gotten out of that stuff." He thought a minute, and added, "Still, I reckon it's better'n getting shot in the butt." Then he laughed again.

It was in Shelby when I first heard the blues. Several boys around there played blues on their guitars. There was Slim Little John, who I played with sometimes, and another guy called Meats Charlie. I even started going with a woman called Dora Martin who was twenty years older'n me. She sang the blues, too. And she was a real good guitarist.

The blues seemed to give me more room for my moods. If I felt good, there was a way of fitting that in. Or, if I was more low, I could get it off me by playing it away. Music was something you could take with you, you know, without no bother. I guess the blues was just part of me, even before I knew it.

Later this fellow in a music store say,
"That harp's already in tune,
you don't have to tune it no more."
I was learnin' by bein' a fool, you know.

1929-1934

Not long before my father got killed, he told me, "Now Sonny, you keep playing that little harmonica you got there, 'cause that'll make a living for you one day. When you get up in the world grown, you got sisters and brothers, but they ain't gonna want to do nothing for you."

He told the truth. And it weren't gonna be too long before I'd find it out.

This one day, Daddy hitched a mule to the wagon and was going into town for a week's groceries. I believe he must have felt something, 'cause most the time he let someone go with him. That day he didn't want nobody along.

He told me and my brother Jaboo, "You all don't have to go. Stay home. I'll see you this evening." He even went by my brother Randel's house and wouldn't let his kids go neither.

Later on, me and Jaboo went over to Slim Little John's house. We was sitting around on the porch playing songs, when this big car pulled up. Mama was inside crying and hollering. I run out to the car and said, "Mama, what's the matter?"

She said, "Come on, son, you daddy's dead. He got run over."

That took all the shit out of me. Jaboo and I jumped in the car and went with them back out to the highway. A truck with a 200 bail cotton load had had a blowout right next to my father and dumped everything right on him. My father weighed 220 pounds and he was mashed flat as a pancake.

Mother took it bad. She couldn't hardly walk by herself for the longest time after that. She'd sit up late in the night, and I'd hear her weeping to herself.

By that time, there was just Jaboo and me at home with mama. So my youngest sister, Lou Daisy and her husband, Clarence Birth, come to help us in the farming. My mother wasn't taking no interest, she didn't hardly cook no more. I helped around wherever I could, hauling the water in and feeding livestock.

Then my youngest brother Jaboo up and got married to a girl called Bertha. He was fifteen and she was only thirteen. It was a pretty small house, so I reckon Lou Daisy and Clarence figured if Jaboo was old enough to get married, he was old enough to do the farming. So they moved away again. That left little young Bertha to do the cooking and she done all right. She cooked pretty good, just mostly learning and all.

Finally it got so my mother didn't want to live in that house no more, with all the memories of my father there. So one day she and Jaboo and Bertha started off walking down the road searching for a new place to stay. I decided to try my luck in the other direction.

When they come in that evening, I had found a house and moved the furniture and had come back for the chickens. I was chasing the little devils around in the yard, when they got there.

My mother said, "Now I know you ain't found no house."

A white man come out the house and said, "Yes, he is, 'cause I helped him move the furniture myself."

That was Mr. Smith, who I'd knowed by way of my father when I'd go to fetch him home from parties he was playing at. Mr. Smith had a house open and used his truck to help me move. We was supposed to pick cotton by the hundred for him and do some plowing and such.

But that farm didn't do so good either and about a year later Jaboo found out about a pretty good farming job near Wadesboro, North Carolina, where his wife's people was from. We decided to split up. Before he left, Jaboo said to me—and I'll never forget him for it—he said, "Sonny, you got more brothers here besides me. All of us can get together and take care of you until you can do better for youself."

I appreciated hearing that and thanked him.

Mother and me were supposed to go to Randel's house but when we got there, he said he didn't want me around. Randel said, "Go out and root for yourself. I ain't taking care of you."

My mother started crying and asked me if she couldn't just fix me something to eat before I left and he told her she better not cook anything for me.

That hurt me. I had a twenty-two pistol in my pocket and I tried to get the hateful bastard outdoors but he wouldn't go. I was going to shoot hell out of him.

Years later, before he died, the lowdown dog was sending up to New York to get money and clothes from me. I wouldn't send him money, but I sent him clothes.

So anyhow, I went over to live with Clarence and Lou Daisy in their little tenant house there near Shelby. It was in the warm summer of the year then. I was getting good with the harp and started playing with a guitar boy called Bill Leach. We kept at it all the time, making music just for ourselves.

In them days, I know now, I had an A harp, but I couldn't tell the difference between an A and B or knowed there was such things. This once I got aholt of a B harp and it about drove us crazy. Bill Leach only played in A and he busted some strings trying to get with me. I most ruined my mouth trying to get to him. We didn't know no better. Later, this fellow in a music store say, "That harp's already in tune, you don't have to tune it no more." I was learnin' by being a fool, you know.

Clarence had changed from the year before. I reckon hard work and no pay can do that sometimes; he was only making thirty cents a day. He'd got so he wouldn't hardly talk to me.

One night, when he thought I was asleep, I heard him complaining to Lou Daisy about me. He said, "Sonny eat too much. Eat all this food and everything and can't see to work."

Lou Daisy told him, "Well, Sonny cuts wood and totes water. He do the best he can. But someday I hope he leaves here so you won't have to be arguing with me about him."

Clarence say, "I hope he does, too."

I laid there thinking, "You stinking bastard, I am gonna leave here and one day you gonna ask me for something." He knew I always kept a pistol with me, so he never would say nothing to me direct, but I was glad to hear how he was feeling. That made me set my mind on going.

The first thing in the morning, I went over to Bill Leach's and told him we ought to get out on our own. Do some playing and try to make us a little money.

Times was hard then and Bill wasn't doing nothing too much, so he was ready to go. Neither one of us had not a damn thing in our pockets, though.

We went back to Lou Daisy's, where Clarence had long since been out in the field. I told her I was leaving and she commenced to crying and hollering. "Where you gonna stay when you get out there and it turns dark?" she asked. "You don't know where to go. . . . A car hit you out there while you trying to hitch-hike or something. . . ."

I said, "Well, I'm leaving here."

I didn't say nothing to her about what I'd heard, but she could see my mind was determined. So she finally give me a quarter out of the seventy-five cent she had on her. It was ten o'clock in the morning when we left out. We walked all the way to King Mountain, about sixteen miles away. We'd decided we'd head for Wadesboro, where Jaboo lived.

We was out in the middle of nowhere, beyond Kings Mountain, when it started getting dark out. I said, "Man, what we gonna do now?"

Bill said, "I know a good place we can stay where nobody won't bother us." Then he led me over to a graveyard he'd seen.

When I started kicking into them stones, I knew where I was. I said, "I ain't staying in here. Wouldn't nothing have to bother me, I'd bother myself to death." I turned around and walked out and he followed.

We went on 'till we come to this lighted filling station. A whole bunch of white fellows was sitting at the front. Bill and I played 'em a couple pieces.

They seemed to get a real kick out of the music, clapping and all. One of them went inside the store and come out with a big bag full of candy and cakes and sandwiches and give it to us. And that was the first I ever earned by way of my music and it felt pretty all right.

The man said to me, "Boy, you out here and can't see good—out hoboing like that—suppose a car run over you?"

I said, "Well, I'm trying to make it."

He said, "It's good you trying to make it, 'cause most bastards won't give you nothing, will they?"

I said, "I reckon not."

The man said, "Here's a dollar. Put this in your pocket. Let the good Lord take a liking of you."

I thought, "Damn, he talking pretty good." I put that dollar in my pocket right fast and thanked him.

He told Bill Leach, "I ain't gonna give you shit, so don't be looking at me that way."

Bill knew I was gonna split with him. We played another piece and then Bill picked up our sack and we headed down into some nearby woods. It was dark sure 'nuff in there. We settled in beside a big tree and ate on some of the stuff from the sack.

I didn't feel too good, but somewhere way in the night I fell off to sleep. Then--Bam!--something fell out of the tree and hit the ground. It sounded like a big ham.

I about tore Bill's shoulder loose waking him to tell him about it. "Man, didn't you hear that?" I asked.

Bill said, "Oh, get on back to sleep. That wasn't nothing but a opossum missed its holt and fell."

I lay listening for awhile and then finally went off to sleep. When we woke up the old roosters was crowing around people's houses. It was good and light then.

We made our way into Gastonia and started playing there 'long side the road. A guy drove up in a great big old truck. He said, "Where you all boys going?"

I said, "Wadesboro."

He said, "I ain't going there. I'm going to Charlotte, though. Crawl in the back and you all can ride that far. Play that harp, though."

We climbed in the back of the truck and played for 'bout an hour, standing up there against the wind. He left us off on one of the side-streets and me and Bill stayed there and made some music for a while. We picked us up two dollars apiece that way.

It was getting 'bout night again, so we went back to the highway. Another truck pulled over. There was a white man driving it, too. He said, "Where you boys headed?"

I told him Wadesboro, and he said, "Who you know down there?"

I said, "A brother named Jaboo."

He said, "Shit, yeah, he can dance his ass off. Lives on J. C. Burch's place. Climb up behind me, I go right by his place."

So we got a ride clean down there. When we jumped down from the back, the man said, "Come into Wadesboro tomorrow and you can make some money. Saturday's a big day there."

We thanked him for the lift and he drove off. Jaboo's house was set back away from the road, in a field. Bill and me went down the path playing our instruments.

My brother come out on the porch and I heard him tell Bertha, "That's Sonny out there playing this harp. I don't know who in the world in on the guitar."

Bill said, "Then go to hell, it's me, Bill Leach."

Jaboo and Bertha laughed and come running down to meet us. They took us inside and made us welcome. Bill had decided he was going to get him a room in Wadesboro. They wouldn't let me. I'll never forget Bertha telling me, "Sonny, you stay here with us and eat what we eat. We're glad to have you." Years later, every time I seen her, I always give her a piece of money for that.

Jaboo was working as a farmhand for wages. He was only making forty cents a day. So, every week-end, I'd go into town and make three or four dollars playing with Bill outside them tobacco plants and warehouses. I'd buy a big ten-pound bag of flour every week and give it to them.

Pretty soon Bill Leach drifted off and I just kept playing in the streets alone. I was getting better and better just by doing it, you know. Sometimes Jaboo would come in with me and stand and watch.

One day Jaboo said, "Sonny, you playing good now. All those people I see around you, you ought to get out and make you some big money."

I said, "That's what I'm gonna try and do."

But I messed up right off. I took a job with this fellow they called Doc. He was a big, old colored guy. He seen the way the crowds gathered around me, so one day he asked me to join him on his medicine show. He was going to pay me three dollars a week. That was big money then.

We hit all the towns around in North Carolina. We'd stay someplace till it'd get to be the week-end, then go out for business.

The first thing, Doc would find some guy and give him two dollars to come around later and act like his stuff cured him. I'd stand out front of the car and play until a crowd of people had gathered 'round. Then old Doc would climb up on the car top with his box of medicine and go to selling it.

He'd say, "This here stuff will cure anything! If you got the headache, just rub a little on your forehead and in two minutes all the pain will be gone! Put it on your shoes, and it'll go right on thru and take that corn out! You take your shoe off the next day and the corn won't even be in there!"

About then, that fella he done paid would come creeping in, complaining about the awful pain he was having. Doc would say, "Step right up here!" and then he'd plant some of it on the fella's forehead.

"How you feel now?" he's ask.

"I don't feel nothing," the guy would say.

People come a-runnin', then. "I got a uncle got the headache! This should help my sister!" They'd be hollering as they come. . . .

Some people'll fall for anything. And that stuff weren't shit. Just some little old wine water he fixed up.

I was around with Doc about a year. Then I started noticing he was holding back on my pay. Two and then three weeks went by and he didn't say nothing about it. And too, I think he'd stole that little twenty-two of mine and throwed it away. I know it was missing not too long after he commenced letting up on my wages. At night I'd hide it in with a little old sack of things I kept of my own.

It was in Greensboro, where Doc lived, that I finally went to him and said, "Doc, you got to give me my money, now."

He said, "I ain't gonna give you shit."

I said, "Well, I'm quitting you, then."

He said, "Goddamn, go. . . !"

So I went on downtown to them tobacco factories and started playin', trying to pick me up a little change to get somewhere with. Some of those local boys told me about a drummer who wanted somebody to stay with his family while he was gonna be gone. So I went to see him.

He explained he was going to New York and needed somebody to stay with his wife and kids. I said, "I can't see any too good. . ."

He said, "I know you can't. But anybody come here, they won't know that. I got a thirty-eight special. Shoot at the first thing you hear come in—don't shoot my wife and kids, though."

I didn't know what he was worried about and never did find out but I was glad to make a little money. I thought he might have something to do with integration, though there wasn't much of it around then that didn't wind up in a killing or lynching.

The next day the drummer left for a two week trip. I had me a little room at the back of the house and kept the pistol under my pillow.

About a week later, on a hot Friday night, I went downtown to a colored restaurant and old Doc was in there. I heard him talking before I got good in the door. I backed out and some fellas told me Doc was reared back inside drinking beer with his wife. So I tore off to the house and got that pistol.

I come back and walked right over to the table where he and his wife was sitting. I said, "Hey, Doc."

"Hey, what the hell do you want now?

I said, "You drinking here, ol' buddy, look like you could give me some of my money."

Doc told me, "I wouldn't give you shit. If you ask me again, I'll knock you off your feet."

I said, "I'll still want my money."

He hit me and knocked me clean under the table. When I come out, his old lady had her shoe off and was hitting me on the head. Then she seen I had a pistol in my hand and she hauled ass.

Doc said, "I ain't scared. Let him shoot," but he was still trying to get away. He had on a pair of white trousers that I could see blurred up in front of me. I shot six times and hit him three in the butt.

I heard a woman yell, "Go get the cops! This blind man's going to kill everybody!"

Meanwhile, Doc lay on the floor hollering like a bull, with all them bullets stopped in his butt. If his old lady had been wearing anything light, I'da shot her too for hitting on my head.

The police come and I told them what Doc had done. One of them said, "You should have killed the bastard."

The policeman wanted to know about the gun. He said, "Where did you get this? Goddammit, there ain't no nigger in the world got a gun like that. I know it must be a white man's."

I was telling them whose it was when the ambulance came screaming up and they took old Doc outside. They carried me down to the station, but the policeman said they weren't gonna lock me up until they'd checked out my story. They called out to the house, and the drummer's wife told them to turn me loose. They told her she had to come down before they could do that.

She drove up in a great big old cadillac and told them how her husband had hired me. Then she wanted to know where the pistol was at. You know how things is done down there. They give her the gun and she drove me back to the house.

The only thing that hurt me was I never did get my pay money back from Doc. . . .

Durham, North Carolina.
Sonny made his living at street playing when he first came to Durham as a young man.

Durham, North Carolina.
Roycroft's, one of the old tobacco warehouses where Sonny would compete with other local musicians.

On Fridays and Saturdays there'd be a lot
of competition. Musicians would come in from
all over lookin' for that payday money.
That's how I come to do all that fannin'
and carryin' on with my free hand;
the more commotion you could stir up,
the bigger crowd you got and the
more money you made.

1934 - 1940

After the drummer come back, he give me twenty-five dollars and said I could go where I wanted. Twenty-five dollars was more'n I ever had before. I bought me my first new suit and that made me feel good. I got me a woman and me and her stayed in a hotel room that night. She had good playing grounds on her and we played all that night.

Next day I rid the bus back to Jaboo's again. I started going back into town on week-ends like before. I figured I just wanted to make an honest living playing my harp anywhere I could. I was thinking on leaving someday, maybe for up North.

One Saturday afternoon I was blowing my harp on a street in Wadesboro when I heard somebody playing a guitar nearby. I said to myself, "Damn, he sounds pretty good."

I sent a boy around to tell him to come over and play some with me. So about the time my boy got to him, he had done sent somebody around to tell me to join him. So I did, and that's the first time I met Blind Boy Fuller.

His voice was rough and hard, and he played a steel-built guitar for that loud mean sound. He just could bring the music out of you. The man was real good and we played a long time together that day.

Later Blind Boy told me he was leaving back for Durham and if I ever come there, to look him up. He gave me his address.

For the next few days I went rambling to Rockingham and Hamlet, around places like that. Then I decided to make it on over to Durham and see Fuller.

I rode the back of the bus into Durham. A boy there at the station took me to Fuller's house on Colfax Street. Fuller invited me to stay with him and his wife, Cora May.

Fuller told me, "I don't have no whole lot of money, but you can stay here with me. I won't charge you no rent. Just chip in and get a little food every day."

And that's what we did, we'd chip our little money in and buy food and Cora May would cook it up. I had a nice little room with a window at the front of the house. It weren't too large, but it was a lot better'n I'd been staying in.

Fuller was a pretty good nice guy. He'd get evil sometime but he was all right to me. I couldn't have lived with him if he wasn't.

Fuller was a grown man before he got blind. He used to work and drive cars and things. They say a woman put poison in a pan and caused him to wash the sight out of his eyes. He didn't tell me that, that's just what I heard.

Blind Boy was a big gambler. He loved to gamble and shoot dice. His brother'd tell him what he'd throwed. Fuller played cards the same way and he used to break people, too. Sometimes he'd break them bad.

I reckon Fuller was one of the jealousest men who ever was. What he couldn't see, he saw anyway. If a cat jumped off a table, he was ready to shoot a man. If he didn't take Cora May with him, he made her stay locked in at home.

Later, after I'd moved in with a woman, he shot Cora May over some fuss they had. He might have been in the wrong hisself, I don't know. But if she's living, she still got a bullet in her now where they couldn't get. She was only in the hospital a small while and then they were together again.

Sometimes I'd play inside the tobacco warehouses where they was sellin' the bundles and sometimes outside on the street. Somebody was always runnin' us off but I'd just wait a little and go back. I recall this one time in front of Currin's I was playin' a little down from some white fiddlers. These cops come tellin' me to move on and this white man stepped out of the crowd just a cussin'. He said, "You son-of-a-bitches, what harm is this man doin'? He ain't beggin'. He's playin' a pretty harp for his money. How come you ain't botherin' them fellas over there? Just let this man alone!" The police didn't bother me no more that day, but the next mornin' that man wasn't there and they run me off again.

One day I was with Fuller and they done the same thing. This cop grabbed Fuller's arm and Fuller pushed it off him. "I'll go," he said, "but don't put your hand on me." Fuller was a big man in Durham but that didn't make no difference to them.

Me and Fuller'd play on the streets every Friday and Saturday. We'd go to Burlington, Greensboro, Winston-Salem, all them places along Highway Seventy. I was just mostly backing Fuller then, singing in a *high-setto*—a falsetto voice—hooping and hollering like they done out in the fields. We were sometimes joined by a fellow named George Washington—"Bull City Red" or "Oh Red"—he had all kinds of names. Played his butt off on a washboard.

On Fridays and Saturdays there'd be a lot of competition. Musicians would come in from all over lookin' for that payday money. That's how I come to do all that fannin' and carryin' on with my free hand; the more commotion you could stir up, the bigger crowd you got and the more money you made.

I found out too, though, that by slapping my palm against my harmonica hand, I could cut the wind off and get a pumping sound. I hear that change dropping, I go to pumping at 'em sure 'nuff.

I was in Durham that I first heard Deford Bailey on the radio, coming off the Grand Ol' Opry. Some of them fellows told me to listen 'cause he was the first colored fellow ever to play on the Opry. He was good, but our styles was different 'cause he played more like country western. I was surprised to hear he had a *Fox Chase* too, but he took the hunter part whereas I took the dogs. I learned *Alcoholic Blues* from him, and some other licks. There was a lot of folks I learned some from, then mixed it on in with mine.

Sometimes, when a good harmonica player hit town, we'd have contests to see who could play the best. They'd come get me and run me to some tobacco shed where they even had judges. Folks would bet money and we'd go at it. I don't recall ever losing, though I may have had to split the take some days. There was a lot of good musicians around in them days but most all of them could see and when things slimmed down too much they'd quit. I didn't have no choice, I had to keep on.

Late that year, I got word that my mama had passed away in Shelby. I was surprised she went on as long as she did. Mama didn't never do too much good after my father died.

I took a bus over and went to the funeral. I was feeling pretty low. I don't know why, but I always get a strong urge to play music at times like that. It gets my mind off trouble some, I reckon.

I seen her buried, then come back to Durham. That night we had a party at Fuller's house and his brother introduced me to a woman called Florence. We had a good time that night and she invited me to live with her over on Grant Street there in Durham. It was two years before I found out Florence couldn't hardly see no better'n me and here I'd been eating her food all that time. Hell, I could have been poisoned. When I found out, I started eating around at the restaurants. It's hard for a blind person to recognize another unless they just start bumping into each other. And that's what we'd been doing.

But, anyway, long before that, me and her ran into trouble over another woman. I met this nice-looking girl on Pettigrew Street, uptown there in Durham. It was a warm, summery evening.

We started talking and she said, "Is that you that plays with Fuller? You ain't Sonny?"

I said, "That's me."

She said, "I live not too far from you. I been wanting to see you."

I told her, "Okay, here I am."

She said, "Why don't you come to my house in the morning about nine o'clock."

I said, "I'll be right there."

We said goodbye and I headed for home. At that time I was letting an old friend board with us, Joe Green. I run into him on the way to the house. He said, "Sonny, I seen you with that pretty girl."

I said, "Yeah, man, I got a date with her at nine in the morning. She lives right up there at that fourth house, that green looking house."

Joe told me, "Man, I know what you gonna do. I wished it was me."

So, while I was at the store later that night, this bastard went right straight and told my old lady that I had this date. Later I found out he even told her how to catch me by holding back and waiting till I had gone up there.

I thought she was kind of quiet when I come home, but I didn't pay it

22

any too much mind. She got in moods sometimes. I just went on to bed.

The next morning I got right up. I was so anxious to meet this woman, I didn't eat no breakfast. I wanted to see this pretty yellow girl. I shot out the house. I didn't know what time it was, but I knew it had to be morning.

I didn't have no idea Florence was following after me. But where she did the wrong thing, she let me get inside the house. Harriet smelled nice, had on a little slip of covering.

We'd just got settled on the bed, when somebody hit the door. Bam! Bam!

I whispered, "Harriet, who's that?"

She said, "I don't know, but don't you open no door."

I told her, "I ain't gonna open no door, don't you worry."

Bam! Bam! It come again.

Harriet grabbed my arm. "Look like they gonna tear the door down," she said.

Then I heard that fool Florence's voice, cracking and hollering on the wood. "I know you in there, Sonny! You in there—come out! If you don't come out, I'm gonna tear this door down!"

I said to myself, "You can tear the door down, but I ain't coming out there."

Bam! Bam! Bam!

Harriet asked me, "What we gonna do?"

I said, "Give me time to get out the back door, then open it to her. But let me get out first."

I got out there on the porch. It was one of them high kind with a bathroom on it. There could have been a well down below—anything—but I jumped anyway. I didn't care, it was better'n letting Florence catch me.

I landed okay, and run under the house. I heard Harriet up there opening the door.

Florence say, "Goddamn, I know my old man's in here!"

Harriet told her, "Ain't nobody been in here, I was just asleep."

"You a goddamn liar. You raggedy-armed son of a gun. I should break your neck."

Harriet was a little scared. She didn't say nothing.

Florence run out on the porch and slammed the toilet room door, looking for me in there. Then she found the side steps and come down them and started off for home.

Some of those guys out there in the street told her, "No, yonder he is, under the house." I heard them talking about the size knife she had with her.

Florence come running back and looked under the house. "Come on out, Sonny!"

I said, "This ain't none of Sonny."

She crawled under inside there and pulled me out, poking that knife around. It was nearabout as long as my arm. I said to myself, "I better go with this fool." There wasn't nothing else I could do 'cause I didn't have mine on me. I was in such a hurry getting gone that morning, I'd left it behind.

We went on back down to the house and passed a few blows and got all right. After she calmed herself down, she told me Joe was the one who had snitched on me. Just then, old Joe come walking into the kitchen.

I told him, "Man, you get your butt out of here!"

He said, "What you mean, Sonny?"

I said, "Get your little rags and go. I thought you was a friend, and here you telling her something to make her start a fuss with me."

The fool answered, "Well, you did tell me that, Sonny."

I had a shotgun in the closet, but I'd borrowed out all my shells a few days earlier, or I'da blowed his sorry self away. I shoved him on out the front door without letting him get nothing, and that was that.

It must have been Fuller who pulled me into the blues sure 'nuff. I'd played with a lot of styles up to that time, but he kind of steadied it you might say. He set it for life the way they was playin' it in Durham around those days. It had a little rag in it, and a washboard bat, and lighter guitar than the blues further on down south. But it could turn dark, too. It could turn anything.

The coming few years, I had me a lot of little businesses going. Fuller and me was still playing on the streets of the 'bacco towns and then during the week, at fish fries and house parties. I'll never forget this night we was playing at this fish fry. Everybody was having a good time when this gal they called Razor-Toting Sally jumped on this guy and started cutting him. She'd cut on a man if he looked at her hard, that's how she come by her name. This fellow was hollering, trying to get loose of her. . . .

Hell, I run off and left my harp behind. Blind Boy run too but he took his guitar. I find out later the man almost died, he was in the hospital nearabouts six months. They never did nothing to Razor-Toting Sally. In those days coloreds could shoot and cut and kill each other and they didn't hardly do nothing about it. But if you hurt a white, you went on the roadgang and had to build his highways for him. So you really come to catch hell both ways.

I was selling liquor back then, too. There used to be a man come around in a truck every Thursday night, selling jars of white corn liquor, you know, getting the sellers stocked before Friday payday. I'd buy me a half-gallon jar for a dollar, and I could make me eight on it. I could pour any size drink a customer wanted. I'd put my finger at the end of the bottle, pointed inside a glass, and when the liquor touched my finger I'd stop pouring. A lot of people came and bought from me, calling themselves helping out.

At the same time I was working at the blind factory across from Pettigrew Street. Great big old brick building that hardly had any windows. We made baskets and chair bottoms and mattresses. I had to work there to get my blind pension, something like $25 a month.

In 1938, Fuller and I went to Chicago and did a couple recordings. *Big House Bound* was one I remember. *Pistol Slapper Blues* was another. I was backing him in a high-setto voice and harmonica.

That same year, a fellow called John Hammond had heard my records and sent me a ticket to come to New York for this thing they was doing called *Spirituals to Swing Concert*. It was in Carnegie Hall—a big old place. Probably the biggest place I ever been to. Bull City Red went with me. They had Count Basie and Benny Goodman and Lester Young on the show, too.

I reckon a lot of 'em thought I was crazy comin' on with my field whoops and hollers but hell, just 'cause you learn music workin' and earnin' on the open street, don't mean it ain't as good as the other. It's still music, ain't it? It's the kind of music that kept a whole lot of folks alive 'cause how others liked it well enough to pay to hear it. Not only money, but it helped them to get over the hard things of their lives.

It was a real nice concert. People yelled and clapped and went crazy over the music. Afterwards, me and Bull City Red took a bus back down to Durham. I commenced doing what I had always done, playing in the streets and at house parties and selling liquor.

Not too many days later, I met Brownie McGhee. It was in Burlington, North Carolina. Fuller and I had gone there on a Saturday to play outside the mills. We was resting on some crates, back of an old wooden store owned by J. B. Long, who was kind of Fuller's manager. He'd got him recording dates with Vocalion.

I'll tell you something about J. B. Long, he had a mean streak in him back in them days. There's two ways of lookin' at a man like that. He helped get people recorded, but he made money on it himself and a lot of times got the copyrights on songs he never wrote. The good he did, he couldn't help but doin' if he wanted to make money. He usually saw to it you got ten dollars a recording but not no royalties.

Fuller threatened to kill him once about money and one time Long threw a ten dollar bill on the ground and told Gary Davis to stick it up his butt. He told me to kiss his butt when I asked for the money he owed me. These things are hard to forget. And what you noticed most was it was you out on the street scufflin', tryin' to get by, not him. You can add that up yourself.

But anyway, old J. B. knew that Brownie was playing there in the streets that day too, so he sent a boy to bring him over. A fellow that owned a stand was letting Brownie sleep in empty taxi cars. When Brownie come, he had a harmonica player with him called Jordon Web.

Brownie and Jordon played apiece and when they was done, Fuller told Brownie, "Man, you can sing all right, but you can't play no guitar."

Brownie always thought hard of Fuller for that. I myself thought Brownie played pretty good for just starting out. He was only about twenty years old then. Brownie must have gone back to his room and practiced. He learned pretty fast. The next time I heard him, he sounded real good.

In the first part of 1940, Fuller went by hisself up to Chicago and cut a record. He sang mostly sad stuff. Songs like *When You Are Gone*, and *Lost Lover Blues*. Uusally, he done songs with more pickup and jump. But not then.

It wasn't but two months later, Fuller went into the hospital with some kidney trouble and died. Never come out from the sleep they give you to operate. It shocked me near to death myself, and a whole lot of others, too. He just didn't seem the kind of guy who would die, not laying down, leastways.

They buried him there in Durham. Then a whole lot of fellows started doing records, using his name—the Friend of Blind Boy Fuller, Blind Boy Fuller's Buddy, Little Boy Fuller. Brownie didn't like it, but they done one calling him Blind Boy Fuller No. 2.

25

About in there, I got an offer to come up to Washington, D.C. to play at a school. Paul Robeson was giving it. Brownie wasn't doing nothing then, so old J. B. Long told him to go along to help look after me, and maybe if they heard him they'd take him, too.

So we got up there and Brownie played a piece and they took him for the program. They was paying Brownie fifteen and me seventy-five. To show you how nice I was, I split up my money with him until we was even. And he'll right now today, say that I never done that. We still get in arguments about it.

Up there was the first time we ever met Leadbelly. He was playing on the same bill. The man could really make that guitar go, too. He told Brownie and me if we ever come to New York, to look him up. I thought maybe I would some day, but I didn't set aside any plans for it then. I haven't never planned too far ahead, or looked for too much. I just take things as they come and do the best I can with them.

After the show, Brownie and I come back to Durham and started playing on the streets together. To this day, we hadn't never signed no contract; we just divide everything even, neither getting more than the other. All that did happen was, I said, "What you think about it? Joining up?" He said, "Well, if you want to, we'll team up together." And that was all there was to it.

Brownie always said he wouldn't never cry, and I got to say I ain't never heard him. He makes the world be right in his own head. Brownie could be standing in the rain, and make the most of the sun. We might fight a lot but I like the guy. You know I got to, or we wouldn't have kept on together. We 'bout like brothers who are different from each other.

Brownie had some trouble at home along in there, and had to take care of it, so we didn't play none for about a week. I used that time to get drunk. Every day I'd go out and not come home till late at night, kicking chairs, kicking dishes off the table, carrying on. That was at 505 Murphy Street. Old Florence kept telling me if I kept it up, she was going to change the door lock. And sure nuff I come in that Friday and couldn't figure out what was wrong with the key. It wouldn't even go in the slot.

I commenced to hollering and hitting on the door, but she never even turned no light on inside. The porch light was on, though, I reckon so I could see enough to leave.

A friend come down there and wanted to know what all the fuss was about.

"She changed the lock on me," I told him.

"You mean you can't get in your own house?"

"I shore can't."

"Well, too bad for you, buddy," he said.

So I went on back to his place and set up all night on a kitchen chair. Next day I went back and fell asleep on the front porch, in a little wicker seat we had out there. Later on she come out and took me back in again. But still, I got a song out of that, my *Change The Lock On The Door.*

Every Monday a whole bunch of us would
have a jam session together. We called it
Blue Monday. There'd be Led, Woody Guthrie,
Pete Seeger, Josh White, and me and Brownie.
We'd buy beer and stuff and sit around
playing all night. People'd come by but we
didn't charge nothing, it was all just for fun.

1940 - 1944

A few days after getting locked out, I got a Special Delivery letter, said they wanted us back in New York for a show. These people had heard us in a concert in Washington. They sent two bus tickets, one for me and one for Brownie. There wasn't no way I could get aholt of Brownie, so I came on to New York and give them Brownie's ticket. They found out where he was somehow, and sent it to him, and he come on up. We stayed at Leadbelly's house then, like he asked us to do.

They was going to do a musical play called *It's All Yours* that Woody Guthrie had wrote. Seems to me it was something about Abraham Lincoln. Something like that. We practised on it for about two weeks.

We was supposed to open on a Friday night, but Woody didn't like what the director was doing to the play so he didn't show up. He was the main man, too. Somebody tried to fill in for him, but didn't none of us know what to do or what we was doing. All we got was laughs. So that killed that; it shut down the same night.

Brownie went up to Connecticut for some deal and I rode back to Durham. She'd changed the lock again and here it was my place, I was paying the rent. She wouldn't open the door, so I kicked it loose and went on in and there they was, standing together.

Florence said, "I been expectin' you, Sonny."

"That why you changed the lock?" I asked her.

Meanwhile, that fellow had slip past, getting near the door. One of Florence's sister's boys come in from the kitchen. He hung out at the house a lot and was crazy about me. He come whispering over to my ear, "Mr. Sonny, that man got your best suit on. He wearin' it now." I'd left three or four behind when I went to New York.

I said to the fool, "You guess you could get out of my suit?" All the while I was moving toward the closet where I keep my shotgun. I heard the door snap shut and he was gone.

Me and the old lady there had some words before we got settled down. She wanted to give me a party the next day, on Tuesday. That sounded good to me. I gave her money to round up liquor and things in the morning.

The next day I decided to go back over to the blind factory so I could keep my pension going. When I got there, the old man meet me right at the door. He was mad 'cause I missed the two weeks. He said, "You fired!" Just like that, no more, "You fired!"

I said, "I don't care, if I'm fired, I'm fired. I'll just go back to New York."

He said, "You should have stayed up there."

"I maybe should have," I told him and then I went on back home. It wasn't too long before the house started to fill up with people drinking and having a good time. Florence had a table all covered with food and liquor.

A little bit later, that same fellow come in still wearing my suit. The same young boy, Ernie Stack, come told me. I went right up to the fool and said, "You got some more clothes, buddy?"

He said, "Yeah, I got more clothes."

I said, "Would you mind to get out of my suit?"

He said, "You say one more word about a suit, I'll knock hell out of you."

I said, "No, you won't," and I backed to the closet and come out with this sawed-off, two barreled shotgun.

He said, "You won't shoot me!"

I pulled both barrels—BOOM!—and to this day I can't figure out how I missed him. Somehow he got thru the front door and closed it and I put a hole in it big enough for a man to crawl in. I went looking for some more shells, and everybody cleared out of the house. So I just stayed in there and drank liquor and ate the food all by myself. Later on I come to be so drunk I just fell in the bed and went to sleep. They sent one of the nephew boys down there to the shotgun. But I was slick enough to keep the shells out so nobody couldn't come in there and blow me away.

The next day I went up to stay with Blind Boy Fuller's wife. Figured since they had the shotgun I'd better keep away for a while. I got my old room at the front back. That very week I got another Special Delivery letter from New York. I have to give Florence credit, she didn't snatch that off. She had it sent to Fuller's house. It was a round of contracts to play at hootenanny concerts.

When I went up to New York this time, I never did go back. They had me and Brownie contracted to go around to various towns with Woody Guthrie—Baltimore, Philadelphia and like that—to play at concert halls. We'd get fifteen a night split three ways. If just Brownie and I went, we'd get seven-fifty each. During the week and in between, Brownie and me was playing on the streets up in Harlem.

Woody got us in a house with a whole bunch of people. It was a big old twelve-roomer on downtown Sixth Avenue. Besides us and Woody, there was Nick Ray, Burl Ives and Beth Lomax. We'd all get together in the morning and chip our money in and get eggs and coffee—we couldn't never afford no bacon. We'd all go out on week-ends and do a little bookin'—made money like that. This kept up until someone got a break, then they'd move on.

One day Led (Huddie Ledbetter) came up there and said to Brownie and me, "You fellows want to come down and stay with me and Baby?"—that's what he called his wife Martha.

I said, "I wouldn't mind."

He said, "I don't have no whole lot, but you all can come down. I won't charge no rent. If you all make any ahead, you can just chip in on the food, give it to Baby."

So we went down there at 306 East 9th Street. We stayed there about two years. Led was playing then at the Vanguard with Josh White; they were a team in those days.

Led weren't like a whole lot of people said. He was a pretty good, nice guy. Me and him got along just good all the time. As far as I go, he was one of the finest men I ever knew.

One thing, he was crazy about women. More crazy than me. And Martha loved him anyway. She was a skinny, dark-skinned woman, loved him to death. To show you how I mean, one night Led was in a hotel with a girl and she run off with all his clothes. He phoned Martha and she come right over with something for him to wear home. That's the way she cared about him. Most women would have stuck a pistol up his nose and cleared his head away.

Every Monday a whole bunch of us would have a jam session together. We called it Blue Monday. There'd be Led, Woody Guthrie, Pete Seeger, Josh White and me and Brownie. We'd buy beer and stuff and sit around playing all night. People'd come by but we didn't charge nothing, it was all just for fun.

During this time, me and Woody and Brownie was still going out together. Woody was one nice guy. You couldn't just tell him from a black guy. He was a straight guy. Woody was from Arkansas; that's why he left there, 'cause he didn't like how them people was going on down there.

Woody had strange ways. He could stay quiet, not saying a word for days on end. I've known him to write songs for hours, one sheet of paper after another. And he'd never stay put in any place too long, not even after he got his own house. He'd pack up and go stay with someone—carrying his whole family—'till they had to ask him to leave. He was always on the move, like he didn't belong no place.

This one time the three of us went down to Baltimore and played for some big shot people, you know. Had a large hall. After we got done playing, they took us all to another little hall and was going to feed us.

So, but they had a small table set way back in the corner for me and Brownie. They wouldn't let us eat with the rest of the people. They told Woody to eat over there with them.

Woody said, "Let's wait a minute. You mean to tell me I had these two guys down here to sing and play—we played together on the stage—and you all enjoyed it—Now we can't sit and eat together?"

The man said, "No, they can't eat over here."

Woody said, "Sonny, you and Brownie go on out. I'll see you at the train station."

We went outside by the door and stood and listened. Woody went over there and turned that big table over and kicked all the food around. We could hear him yelling, "You goddamn bastards, pick it off the floor and eat it and pay for it, too!"

During that time, we did about two weeks of recordings for Mose Asch. It was Cisco Houston, me and Woody and Brownie. He paid us all ten dollars a night. He wasn't giving no royalties, that was it.

Brownie moved up to Harlem in late 1943. He got a room for me right across the street from him at 110 East 125 Street. Along about in there, the bookings got kind of slim, and me and Brownie took to the streets again, picking up what change we could.

Brownie and I made some recordings for a fellow by the name of Marty Schaft. He paid us forty cents for the album. I don't know if it ever come out. I couldn't even tell you what label it was.

We used to hit the streets on Friday and Saturday, and sometimes we'd made near about a hundred dollars. That was big money then. You could get a pretty suit for twenty-five. We'd come out Sunday, dressed up with a necktie and such, and sit in a bar and drink all day.

People used to ask, "Where you all work at?"

They didn't know we'd been out on the concrete hustling like hell. Harlem was different then. You could lay on the street or sit on your stoop and go to sleep and wouldn't nobody bother you. You sit there with your money in your pocket and that's where it'll be when you wake up. Now you ain't hardly safe in the daytime out walking.

I met Roxie, my first wife, early in 1944. I was down to Ledbelly's house one day and she was there. Sis was staying with another guy at that time but they wasn't doing too good. She was originally from Williams, North Carolina. I found out she was earning her way cooking for some people downtown. Siss was older'n me, maybe by twenty years.

We got along real good. So when she and her old man separated, she come looking for me. Started staying with me in that little room I had uptown there.

One evening me and Brownie was playing at 126th Street and Lenox, when this real tall fellow come up to us. He asked if we'd come down and play some tunes for his sister-in-law, who was very sick. So we went over to her room and played quite a few numbers for her. She was happy to hear us.

Afterward, the man walked outside with us and thanked us. We wouldn't take no money. He introduced himself as Alec Seward. Alec asked if Brownie wouldn't teach him some chords and Brownie agreed. Alec turned out to be one of the best friends I ever had in my life. Years later, when I got back sick, he'd come and see me every day, helped lift me around, cooked, did everything he could.

Alec was working then on the docks, as a longshoreman. He'd played quite a bit down south before coming up north. I liked the way he sang. Alec had a gruff, lonesome sounding voice but he just couldn't get no jobs singing for pay. I don't think he tried all that much because he wasn't nobody to care much about being known. He learned a lot from Brownie but he only put it to use at private house parties.

But like I was saying, Brownie and me left Alec at his sister-in-law's place. We was on the way home, when this guy run up to Brownie and pushed him down. I hurried over and said, "What's the matter with this guy, Brownie?"

Brownie said, "He's playing."

I said, "A man playing, gonna push you down like that?"

So Brownie went to trying to get up and the guy'd shove him down again.

Left to right—Brownie McGhee, B. B. King, Sonny Terry and Alec Seward.

With the Seeger family, 1958. Pete is on banjo, Tanya is on his lap and Miko is entering the house.

I told the guy, "Man, stop that bullshit!"

He said, "I'll push *you*."

He grabbed hold of me and I give him a left to the jaw and he went down. So I jumped down on him with my carpet knife. I was going to do it to him. A crowd gathered quick and I heard some fellow say, "Aw, I told you that man could see. Look at him, he's fixin' to cut that man."

A whole bunch of people grabbed me before I could hurt him. The man hurried off like a scared rabbit.

Me and Brownie felt kind of off after that, and we didn't feel like playing no more. So I decided I'd go over to see this girlfriend I had on the side.

Hell, I wasn't there five minutes before she started pickin' at me about this and that. See, she wanted to get rid of Roxie and let her move in. I wouldn't do it. Roxie was my main woman. It wasn't nothing but one room, but still, Siss kept it nice you know, kept my clothes clean and all.

Betty kept arguing, raising her voice at me. I told her to shut up or I'd go up the side of her head.

Her voice turned sweet. She said, "You know better'n to hit me."

I said, "I'll hit anybody. Don't tell me that I won't hit you now."

Then I give her a smack on the face. She went down and come up and that was all she wrote. Gawd, she was all in my face, scratching and going on like a mad woman. I would have cut her but she wouldn't let me get my knife out.

Somehow or another I made it to the door and got away. When I come in that night, I told Siss I got all them scratches trying to help Brownie out of that situation. I figured as long as I had 'em, I might as well make myself look good.

Sonny and his first wife, Roxy.

I'm mostly my music, and I don't think the life
I've lived means anything special, but sometimes
you get the urge to tell about it.
I don't hate nobody, I can say that.
And I have to say most people been real nice to me
except for one guy down in Greensboro, N.C. years ago
who stuck his hand in my hat and stole out a dollar.
I hope the fool's still spending it.

1944-1968

For a long time there we didn't get much bookings. We'd just play the streets. In those days we passed everything in the street but a liquor store. We did a couple years like that, pulling in change money on week-ends, paying the rent, on like that.

Now up until that time I ain't never done no singing, just that high-setto and whooping. I was backing Brownie like I done with Fuller. It's kinda funny how I did come to sing.

Brownie had him several women and somebody told one of them something that caused a fuss between two of them and put Brownie in the middle. He thought I done it, and stopped talking to me. We lived right across the street from each other and he'd pass me by without saying nothing. Alec come over a lot and he'd tell me when Brownie come out but I never heard no words from him.

That was early in the week, so I got to thinking maybe he wouldn't want to go out with me on the week-end. I needed the money so I decided I'd better try to sing in a regular voice. I never thought I could. But when I tried, it sounded pretty good. I sang *Crow Jane* and *John Henry*, some like that. I kept at it, doing some of Fuller's songs, too. Brownie wouldn't never do any of Fuller songs, 'cause he didn't want nobody comparing 'em.

Come Friday, Alec and I was sitting out on the front stoop. He was playing and singing when Brownie come out. He stood there for a long time, saying nothing. Then he come easing over to where we were.

"You want to go out play some tonight, River?" he asked me.

I said okay. But when we got out, he was surprised to see I was singing, too. And ever since then we've split the songs up even, him doing half and me doing half. I reckon Brownie wished he'd never believed bad in me, then he could be the only star today.

Then one night we was playing up on 128th Street, between Lenox and Fifth, and somebody dropped a gallon jug of water at us. Brownie had on a hat with a brim on it, and it hit through the brim. If the jug had hit his head, it would have busted his skull open.

Brownie said, "Horse, this is it. We just gonna quit now."

So me and him stopped playing in the street. We did some recordings for Mose Asch, for ten dollars a shot, just to carry us along. That same year, they was putting on a show downtown called *Finian's Rainbow*. There was a special part in it for a harmonica. They'd had about twelve different guys and couldn't none of them make the grade.

This fellow Paul Robeson had something to do with the show. He looked in his book and seen my name. He told them, "I know a guy just fit the part."

They looked in the phone book and I just had had a phone put in that year. One of them called me up.

The man said, "Come down, Sonny. We want to put you in a show."

I said, "I don't know how to get down there."

The fellow said, "Just tell me where you're at and we'll come pick you up."

"I'm living at 110 West 126 Street," I told him. "A little apartment room there. Just ring three bells and come on up."

They come around and asked me if I knew any other bluesmen. I gave them a whole list. They had a whole bunch come down for the audition—Brownie, his brother Sticks McGhee, Bob Harris and another couple more guys.

What they was mainly looking for, though, was a harmonica player. They had a record there of mine with me doing whooping things like *Lost John*. They played the record and afterward, the guy say to me, "Sonny, the script read like this. What we want you to do is play just like you done on the recording. Can you do the same thing like that every night for three minutes?"

I said, "You mean the exact same way?"

He said, "Yeah, it's got to be that way."

I said, "No, I can't do that."

He said, "Well, you got to."

I said, "It always come out different, according to how I feel. I can't help it." I kept telling him over and over how I couldn't do it. He said I had to.

Finally, I asked him how much he was intending on paying me.

The man said, "Three hundred a week."

I liked to faint. I'd never made no money before as much as that. I hurried up and told him, "Oh hell, yeah, I can do it the same way every night."

So he gave me the job. Didn't none of the others get work there. Brownie started up a little band and played over in New Jersey. Me and him was still partners, but we always said if one gets a chance to make it, go on ahead. If he'd got the job in Finian's instead of me, there wouldn't have been nothing I could say. Just wished him well and found something on my own.

The Finian show did two weeks in Philly before coming on in to New York. Then we played in the city for two whole years and at the end of them I was making five hundred a week. That was the first time in my life I was making enough to save some. The show done nine months on the road and even a couple years away from that, we done summer's off things.

Now see, the show only played six days a week. We was off on

A publicity photo for *Finians Rainbow,* Sonny's "big break."

Sundays, and I'd get myself stupid drunk. Come in on Monday and couldn't hardly get no high-setto off my voice. Man say, "Sonny, why you got to drink so hard? You come in here sounding like a frog with its nuts out." But you see, I hadn't never changed nothing for music . . . I didn't know how. 'Cause it was me and I felt like getting drunk on Sunday.

In 1948, at the age of thirty-seven, I got married to Roxie. I been asked why, as we was already living together. I reckon it was just I wanted to be married, too. All my brothers and sisters had done it.

I was pretty drunked up at the ceremony. To tell the truth, I don't recall it at all. Siss just told me next morning, in that little room, that I was her husband. I said, "If you shore I was there, I reckon I am." She laughed good.

Siss was one fine woman. She just couldn't read and write good or take care of my business. I wished she could have. I probably would have done a whole lot better, not made so many mistakes. But I'll tell you this, what I liked about her was that the whole time I had her, I never catched her going after another man or nothing. That meant a lot to me. And she wasn't none of them pocket-picking women. What I had in my pocket was safe as far as she went.

The only thing she ever give me trouble on was my drinking. She didn't like to see me drink none. She was a lot religious. The only sin she done against the church, was smoke. Siss couldn't never quit that and I think it hurt her health later on.

After *Finian's Rainbow*, Brownie was still playing over in New Jersey, so I just rested for a while, living off what I'd saved.

Me and Alec and Siss used to travel a lot down to Led's place and sit around and play together. Martha'd fix us up good food. Led had been in the hospital not too long before and come out still not knowing what he had. At that time one of his toes wouldn't bend and he had a foot problem; he was walking with a cane, dragging one leg.

I think it was in the June of that year, 1949, when he suddenly had no use of himself. He couldn't hardly swallow or hold his head up. Led had lost down to hardly nothing; his arms got like a little child's.

They took him into Bellevue about in November but even then Led always thought he'd be coming back out. What they found he had I don't guess there's more'n two or three people could say it.* It killed off all his muscles. We visited him and he wouldn't never give up hope on himself; he was hard at letting go.

It was in the cold of the year, in December, on the 6th I think, when Led passed. It 'bout struck me down. He died a poor man. Here all these people loved to hear him sing and play and he died hardly a cent in his pocket. It hurts you, and makes you a little scared about yourself, too.

After the first of the year, Brownie and I got together again and started bookin' ourselves at ten dollars a night, split even. These were mostly club dates. We also played at rent parties and fish fries and barbecues. We done that until 1955, doing whatever little thing we could get. I spent everything I had saved. I was down low to nothing all over again.

*Amyotrophic Alteral Sclerosis

Around about then, somebody contacted Brownie on this play they was getting ready to do called *Cat On A Hot Tin Roof*. They wanted him to bring musicians down to them. Brownie brung a whole bunch except for me. On that day I was off drunk, getting in trouble.

They told Brownie what kind of songs they wanted. There was a part in there for a harmonica, and after Brownie studied it a while, he told them, "The only person I know can do this, is Sonny Terry." That's how I got the job.

Brownie and I both played in *Cat*. We was in it for two years in New York, then we carried it on the road for eight months. When we come off *Cat*, we still didn't have no future but we thought we was a little better than to play on the streets.

That year Big Bill Broonzy was booked to go to England to do some concerts, but he had a throat operation and couldn't make it. So he asked us to take his place. They sent us the contracts and it was the first time I'd ever been out of the country. The folks over there were crazy for our music. They done some good paying, too. We did that same trip to Europe pretty near every year. A whole lot of blues guys just stayed over there, because they was treated so good. They were treated better'n they were in their own country.

After we come back from England, I went out booking awhile with Pete Seeger and Brownie got him another band and worked it in New Jersey and places.

Pete had him an agent named Endicott. He was glad to get any work he could after that communist thing he was in, but what I didn't know was the bastard Endicott was taking fifty percent of everything Pete was making. The reason to me not knowing, was Pete was paying me. I reckon Pete wasn't in position to complain.

I took Siss on some of them trips with me. She used to love to travel. I took her to California, Minnesota, Washington—all around. To the end of her life, she never did forget that. Even when her mind was gone and she was in a home, she used to tell everybody about them travels.

So, being Endicott was taking so much out of Pete, Pete asked me one day if Brownie and I didn't want to sign him direct. Pete figured that way I could make more; he felt the man was taking such a chunk because he was chancing his own reputation.

That was back when people never called out their beliefs like now too much. Pete was a good guy and couldn't help but be. There wasn't nothing more important to him than doing the right thing. I'd have to say Pete Seeger to be one of the finest men I've ever knowed.

Brownie and I hadn't never had no agent before. The onliest thing we ever got, was what people felt like giving us. So we jumped at a chance to sign with him. We didn't know until later that we had signed a contract for fifteen damn years and the man was taking twenty percent of everything we made. When we spoke on it, he said that's what all agents got and we didn't know no better.

We didn't half know what we were getting into. He'd book us all over the country and when we'd get done playing, they'd tell us, "We sent the check to Mr. Endicott." The bastard would take the check, mess around

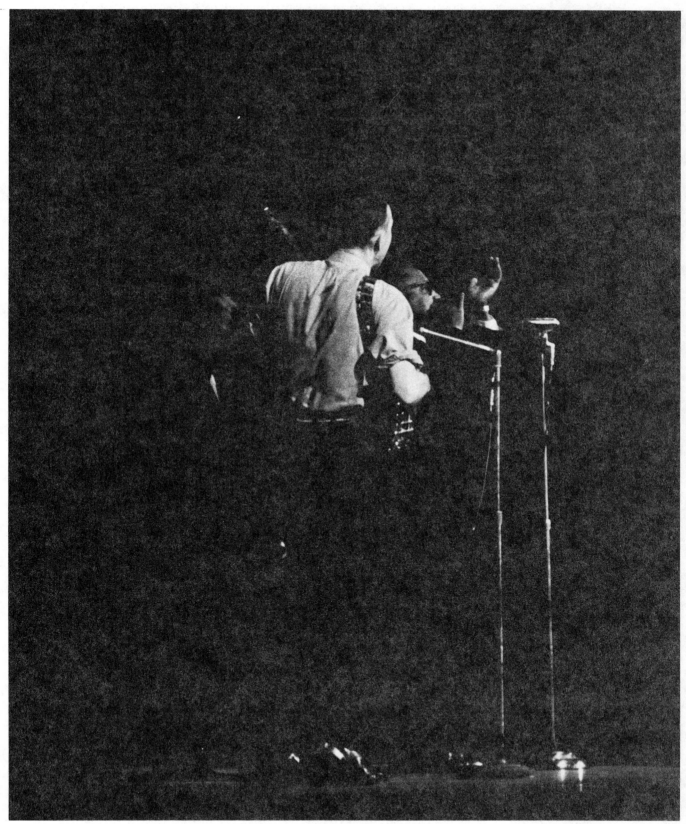

Pete Seeger and Sonny at Carnegie Hall, 1958.

Sonny Terry and Brownie McGhee.

with it, take out this and that and give what was left to us. He'd sign our names to the contracts so we'd never know what we was supposed to get anyway. There was times when we never knew where we was due next; we'd call him to find out and he'd charge the call against our checks. We'd complain and he'd say, "Write a letter." There was even one time in Chicago when the ass invited us out to dinner in a big old place. Me and Brownie ordered up everything we could think of: T-bone steaks, pie with ice cream on it—everything.

When we got done eating and was all stuffed up, the dirty rascal told us to pay for our own food. I liked not to have had enough money to pay mine; I was digging in my pockets, trying to scrape it together.

But even with all that, we hung on a long time. I reckon it was because we was getting work, even if we was being cheated. We kept on fussin' at him about this or that. Brownie'd say, "River, this bastard ain't right." I'd say, "Well, maybe the bastard'll do a little better."

But it got so he wasn't even giving us enough to travel on. It was in Winnipeg, Canada, when I finally told Brownie I was through. I told him I'd go home and live on relief 'fore I'd let this guy take narry another cent.

That very same day we got a contract in the mail from Harry Belafonte, who we'd known years before when he used to come around our places in Harlem to listen to us play. He had him a big name by then. Brownie read on the contract where Endicott was supposed to get one-half of everything we made. I hurry and called Harry's manager up and told him not to send Endicott nothing until we got there. And he didn't.

Harry was paying us two hundred and fifty dollars a week for rehearsals before going on tour with him. This guy tried to get in on that and Harry told him he didn't have nothing to do with it; he didn't have us under no contract. So where Endicott fouled hisself up, was he sued Belafonte. So Harry had to take twenty percent away from our pay and put it in escrow until the thing got settled. It was in the court for years and we finally won.

That same year, me and Roxie moved down to 85th Street. By then my wife had gotten real worse. I had to hire a girl called Quincy to look after her. I didn't know how they was mistreatin' her until years later when my neighbor, Kent Cooper and some others, told me. They'd give parties and raise hell all night and hardly feed her. They was spending what money I could send back for having fun. My step-daughter, Annabelle finally come in there and threw the whole bunch out.

But anyway, going back, things wasn't so bad when me and Brownie commenced playing with Belafonte all over the country in 1962. He helped us get in with another agency, APA, who started looking after us pretty good.

Things run pretty smooth until 1967 when my wife died and I got pretty sick myself with arthritis. Didn't nobody think I was going to pull out of it but I did.

I met a good woman, named Emma, in 1968, and my life went right sure 'nuff after that. It's hard to find a woman who pulls with you instead of against you. Emma was what I always wanted. She could help me and she was small built and I love her. I feel real lucky in getting her.

I'm mostly my music, and I don't think the life I've lived means any-thing special, but sometimes you get the urge to tell about it. I don't hate nobody, I can say that. And I have to say most people been real nice to me except for one guy down in Greensboro, N.C. years ago who stuck his hand in my hat and stole out a dollar. I hope the fool's still spending it.

I don't know what it would have been like had I been able to see. Better or worse. But I got a song that goes,

> *Some people say, "Seeing is believing."*
> *That's the story they always tell me.*
> *Well, I can't see love but I can feel it.*
> *Yes, you know that's good enough for me.*

So, I reckon for me, that's about get it.

Blues Harp Basics

If you've decided you want to learn to play the blues harmonica, one of the first things you might ask is, 'How did the great ones learn, how did Sonny Terry learn to play?' The most important thing to understand about blues harp is that all the masters were self-taught. There were no schools, no books, no teachers. They learned by listening, experimenting, and discovering new sounds.

This is particularly true for Sonny Terry. Although his father first showed him how to hold the harp and single out notes, he went on, in essentially total isolation from other influences, to develop perhaps the most original style of country blues harmonica. Sonny speaks of the effect his accidental blindness had on his playing in his early years: "Well, if it hadn't been for my blindness I don't think I'd have come this far with the harp." Sonny says that following the accident to his second eye, he "stayed in the house for two whole years, wouldn't even come out, just played and practiced with my harp." While Sonny's blindness certainly deepened his love and devotion to the harp, the important thing to bear in mind here is the value of spending a whole lot of time by yourself if you want to learn. This book, in part, attempts to assist you in learning Sonny's music. But you must learn by yourself!

Although this section of the book is not meant for the beginner, a few basics about the harp are in order.

Structure of the Marine Band Harmonica

If you've been playing the harp for a while, you probably know that the best harp you can buy is a *Hohner*. Sonny, along with almost every other top blues harp man, plays the *Hohner Marine Band Model Number 1896*. It is a diatonic harp (based on the eight-tone scale — the white keys on a piano) with ten holes and twenty reeds. Hohner makes them in all the keys of the chromatic scale (twelve tones — all the black and white keys of the piano), but for the sake of learning Sonny's style, the A and B♭ harps are the best. They are the ones he uses for most songs, and their deeper resonances are well suited to Sonny's frequent use of rhythmic chord phrases.

This diagram of the A harp shows you the tunings of the twenty different reeds. The key signature of the harp (A) is the note you get when you blow into the #1 hole. This is true for all Marine Band harps, regardless of the key. The B♭ harp will give you a B♭ when you blow on the #1 hole, as will the #1 hole of all respectively keyed harps.

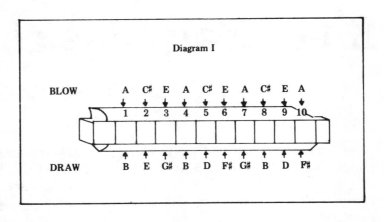

Diagram I

The diatonic harmonica is designed to be played in the key of its signature. To play in the key of C, you would select a C harp; in the key of A, an A harp, etc. This is called the *straight harp* position. If you blow on holes #1 through #4, you get an A major chord; 4 through 7 and 7 through 10 also give you an A major chord. By blowing or drawing on single notes you get all the notes you need for Western, European, and diatonic melodies. Things are made fairly simple for you, see? After all, Hohner was a German, and the music that the harmonica was designed for was European. Not to put this music down, but what happens if you want to play the blues?

You may know already that almost all blues on the Marine Band is played in what is termed the *cross-harp* position. With very few exceptions, all of Sonny's music is played in this position. What this means is that instead of playing in the key of A on an A harp, Sonny plays in the key of E. This puts him on the #2 hole draw or the #3 hole blow for his tonic (that tone which the tune revolves around and always seems to come back to). The advantage of this position is that almost all the notes you use lie on the draw reeds, and it's the draw reeds that give you that deeper tone and the opportunity to *bend* or *slide* your notes. In this postion, you still have access to good chord work, with the E major tonic chord on holes #2 through #4 *draw* and the subdominant A major chord on holes #1 through #4 *blow*. These chords are important to remember. Sonny makes much use of them, especially in his hootin' blues and train songs which we'll talk about later.

But the main point to remember here is that M. Hohner never conceived the diatonic harp to be played in this *cross-harp* blues fashion. Somewhere along the line somebody found you could slide or bend the natural vibrating tone of the reeds (as labeled in Diagram I) to get those notes that are missing from the diatonic scale, thus making the Marine Band essentially a chromatic instrument. Later on, we'll get into how the design of the diatonic harp determines the different natures of these bends from hole to hole. For now, it's enough to understand that the *cross-harp* position and the vocal-sounding, sliding bends that typify it, was a fortunate discovery but an unintended by-product of M. Hohner's design.

44

Holding the Harp

Staying basic for a while, the first thing to consider is how to hold the harp. There are different ways to hold it, and no one way is correct. Most people probably pick up the harp with the hole numbers facing up. This puts the lower or bass end of the harp on your left. Sonny holds his harp with the bass end on the right and the numbers facing down (the way his father showed him originally). He says: "They tell me that's wrong, you know. If it is, I don't wanna be right. See, if I hold the bass on the left, and then I start to move on the harp, well, then I ain't got nothin' left down there!" Whichever way you prefer, grip the harp firmly with the thumb and index finger of one hand and use the other hand to form a tight cup around the rest of the harp. (See Diagram II).

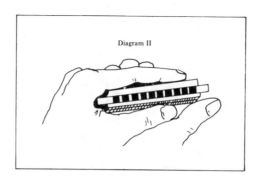

Diagram II

This cup will certainly take some time to develop, but the importance of the hands cannot be overemphasized. Try to seal off all the openings between hands and fingers in much the same way as you would when cupping the hands to hold water. The idea is not to seal off the sound, but to prepare this tight little chamber for opening at the right time and in the most effective manner. A good tight cup when even slightly opened at the right time will double or triple the volume of the harp. Experiment with different ways of opening this cup. You may choose to lift just one finger or several. You can also open the lower or palm end of the cup, pivoting from, and keeping closed, the finger or top side of the cup.

It's best to have the bass end toward the gripping hand. This will put the lower tone reeds (#1 through #4) well in the center of the cup. These reeds are the ones that respond best to the various effects you can get with your hands. Of course, much depends on the size and shape of your hands, so in the long run, whichever is most comfortable for you is right.

Just remember, though, that in playing Sonny's style, you must support the harp with one hand, leaving the other free to smack or fan the harp at any time. Some harp players support the harp with both hands. This is adequate for amplified playing (harp and microphone cradled together in hands), where the hands are used differently, but for acoustic work it doesn't leave one hand free to get those nice slapping and fanning effects.

One of the fascinating things about the blues harp is the many different ways there are of making the same sound. You can hold the harp with numbers facing up or down, gripping with the left hand or with the right, and still make that same beautiful sound. *It's not important if you want to play Sonny's style, to hold the harp upside down.* In the same way, there are different ways to single out notes and still get the same basic sound.

There are two basic ways to single out notes. In the first, you let your mouth rest on the harp, lips covering three or four holes. Then you place your tongue on the harp and block out all but one hole. You may place your tongue on either the right or left side, but the remaining side of your mouth along with your tongue serves to block out all but the one hole. One advantage of this method is that the tongue can be used as a percussive tool by beating on and off the harp and punctuating each note that is singled out. In addition, many bluesmen who play amplified harp employ this *tongue blocking* method because it allows for a tighter seal around the harp and microphone. When blocking with the tongue, the mouth is spread over a wider area of the harp, thus maintaining the tight cup between hands and face that is essential to good response from the amplifier.

The second way to single out notes is by centering down on one hole using only your lips. In this method, the tongue remains off the harp and the lips do all the blocking out. This is the way Sonny singles notes. This method leaves his tongue free to achieve various flutter and trill effects, and in combination with his hands to cut off the sound for percussive "pops". For this reason, it's important that you try this method of singling if you don't already use it. You may wish to combine both ways of singling notes by alternating between each in playing riffs. But some knowledge of singling using only the lips is essential to learning much of Sonny's music. Again though, whichever way you have found to be most comfortable is best for you. So, don't spend a lot of time changing your approach. Remember, everyone's lips and tongues are different, and there's more than one way to make the same sound. Learn by yourself.

One of the great problems in learning the blues harp is the difficulty of achieving and maintaining a clean and natural tone on all the different holes of the harp. This is especially true for the draw reeds. For instance, many people are able to single out a good clear tone on the #2 hole blow reed. But few find it easy at first to get a good natural tone on the #2 hole draw reed. This is because in their attempt to single out the hole, they are narrowing down the opening of the hole with their lips and constricting the flow of air. This sucking action changes the natural vibrating tone of the reeds and results in what is called a *bend*. This may be more of a problem to those who single holes with their lips. In narrowing down the opening of the lips, they block off a portion of the hole on either the top or bottom, and often leave the sides of the hole unblocked (see Diagram III). This often results in a slur of more than one note.

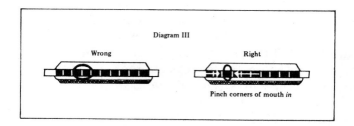

Diagram III

Wrong   Right

Pinch corners of mouth *in*

Of course, there are some times when you might want to get such a slur. But if you're playing single notes, the key thing to understand is that there are no reeds above or below the hole, just the mouthpiece. The problem is to narrow your lips along the vertical axis. Once you get the entire hole cleanly singled out in this manner, the rich, natural tone of the draw reeds will come easily.

Bending Notes

What about *bending*? To play the blues on the harp you must know how to *bend* or *slide* the tones on the reeds. There are different ways to do this, but they all involve one principle: *If you constrict the flow at any point along its passage from reeds to lungs you change the resultant pitch of the reeds*. Most harpmen *choke* the harp to achieve this effect. They narrow the opening in their throats to constrict the air flow. Some who single out holes with their lips are able to constrict the flow by partially blocking the hole with their lips or *squeezing*. Others who *tongue-block* let their tongue partially block the hole they are singling. In all these techniques, there is a simultaneous increase in pressure from the lungs. You must blow or draw harder to get the bend. Sonny uses both the choking and the squeezing technique to bend notes. He chokes the hole on #1, and #2, and #4 draw, and squeezes for the bends on the #3 draw. We'll see shortly why he does this.

Below is a chart representing the holes of the Marine Band A harp showing all the notes possible to attain by either blowing, drawing, or bending.

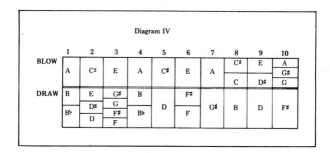

Diagram IV

	1	2	3	4	5	6	7	8	9	10
BLOW	A	C#	E	A	C#	E	A	C#	E	A
								C	D#	G#
										G
DRAW	B	E	G#	B		F#				
			G		D		G#	B	D	F#
	Bb	D#	F#	Bb		F				
		D	F							

47

The notes listed *at the top* of each draw or blow box are the natural tones, *without any bend*. Notes listed below these are the tones you get when bending, or constricting in varying degrees. Notice in particular the number of notes that are possible to get in the #2 and #3 draw holes. The #2 gives you one natural tone (E) and two bent tones (D♯ and D). The #3 draw gives you one natural tone (G♯) and three bent tones (G, F♯ and F). It's easy to see that these holes require much attention. Control of the constricting process is very critical here. Too much pressure and you bend the note too far. Too little pressure and you don't bend down far enough. Many harpmen, including Sonny, choose to squeeze the harp on the third hole rather than choke because of the greater control this technique offers here. Whatever technique you employ to bend, it's a good exercise to sit down at the piano and try to practice these different full and partial bends by matching the tones on the harp with those on the piano. In this way you will develop the right feel in your lips or throat for each tone on these bends. This feel is essential in playing almost all blues riffs. In moving from one hole to the next you must have your mouth and throat prepared for the exact tone that you want.

The more you play, the more you will begin to understand that each hole on the harp (and I mean primarily the draw reeds) is like a separate axe. You cannot simply learn to play the #2 draw reed and expect to apply what you've learned to playing the #4 draw reed. A saxophone player has much more the same feel in his mouth from note to note than does a harp player. He has only one reed. But the Marine Band has twenty reeds. Why do they behave so differently from each other?

As I mentioned earlier, the specific design of the Marine Band as a diatonic instrument has much to do with this. Look again at Diagram IV and notice that the *distance* in tone between the blow and the draw reeds (natural tunings—no bends) of any particular hole is not consistent throughout the harp. On the A harp, there is only one note (B♭) between the blow (A) and draw (B) reeds in the #1 hole. But there are two notes (D and D♯) between the blow (C♯) and draw (E) reeds of the #2 hole. And the third hole has three *missing* notes (F, F♯, and G) between the blow (E) and the draw (G♯) reeds.

All these *missing* notes, of course, are the tones you get when bending. It's interesting to notice that when bending on the harp, *both the blow and draw reeds are vibrating*, and both are essential to the resultant note. The note that you get when bending is a kind of resolution of the natural blow and draw tones of the hole. What this all means is that the nature of the feel of these bends is not always the same from hole to hole, and the feel of the draw reeds, whether bending or not, is equally as various across the harp.

Some similarities do exist between different holes on the harp, however. While the #2 hole and #3 hole are completely unique, holes 1, 4, and 6 are quite similar in feel. The tone *distance* between blow and draw reeds in these holes is the same (see Diagram IV). They all have only one note that you can bend to. And, in a sense, they are easier to deal with than holes #2 and #3, primarily due to this point. While it requires more pressure to get the bend, (and thus results in a louder sound), you don't have to worry about *partial bends* as you do with holes #2 and #3. No matter how much pressure you exert on the bend, once you've got it, you can't bend down any farther.

While the draw reeds and the bends you can get from them are the most important for blues, there do exist some blow bends on the harp that are used in the blues. The technique is different here, although the principle of constriction still applies. Holes 8, 9 and 10 (blow) can be bent by pursing the lips tightly together over the hole and placing the tongue in an arched position close up against the portion of the palate just behind the front teeth. The constriction takes place between the arched portion of your tongue and the front palate. You must blow much harder as you narrow the passage between these two. The result is a very loud, shrill sound. This type of bending is used mostly in the *straight harp* style where entire solos are frequently played on holes #7 through #10. However, Sonny uses the #9 hole bend to punctuate a phrase in cross-harp position. The shrill pop is an excellent contrast to the deeper tones of holes #1 through #4, which are the core of the cross-harp style.

Sliding Notes

In the preceding discussion of bending, much emphasis has been placed on the ability to reproduce the note intervals of the chromatic scale (the scale represented by all the white and black keys in one octave on the piano). Holes #2 and #3 were mentioned as especially important because there are points along the bends on these holes that correspond to several different notes on the piano. But the harp as it is played in the blues, functions much more as a vocal type instrument, rather than one like the piano, which plays an organization of notes, of points within a discontinuous scale of tones. The harp is vocal. It is like a guitar or a horn. It can slide in a continuous manner from one note to another. So, while in some blues riffs you might simply employ a note that lies somewhere along a bend, in many cases you might also slide up to or down from that same note.

For instance, instead of playing the two separate notes B♭ and B (#4 hole draw bend and #4 draw natural—A harp), you may wish to let your bend (B♭) slowly ease up to the B. By gradually reopening the constriction and letting the pressure off, you can get sort of a crying sound. This same sliding effect can be obtained on all the different bends of the harp. You can slide down the bend as well as up. A down slide Sonny uses as part of many riffs starts on G (#3 hole draw bend) and slides down the bend to F♯ (#3 hole bend). But notice how the slide starts on a partial bend and goes down to another partial bend and no further. Sonny knows exactly where that G and that F♯ lie. He's developed the feel in his mouth for all the notes from G♯ down to F, so he knows how to prepare for the G and when to stop sliding precisely at the F♯.

Perhaps much of the foregoing material seems very elementary to those readers who already have some experience with the blues harp. There are other, more advanced techniques such as vibrato, trilling and conservation of wind which we could deal with. But this is not primarily an instruction book on the blues harp in general. The fundamentals presented have been fashioned as an introduction to the blues harp styles of Sonny Terry. And, if you want to play in Sonny's style, you always have to go back to the basics. His command of all the techniques on the harp is so total that his body, his mouth, and his lungs have a complete understanding of the harp, over and above anything that can be written or spoken of. There can be a real danger in conceptualizing too much about the harp. While it may be an aid to some people, there's no substitute for playing. So let's get down to learning some of Sonny's things.

The Tablature System

The following system will be used to transcribe Sonny's music. Bear in mind that this system, or any system, including script, has its shortcomings. Music is sound. It can never be adequately represented on paper. For this reason, we've provided a record insert with this book which corresponds to the tabs.

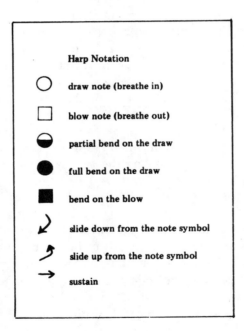

The above symbols will be placed in the following table to indicate from which holes the different blow, draw, bend or slide notes are obtained. The numbers on the left are the hole numbers of the harp, and the columns will denote the measure of time, or *note value* (how long a note should be played in relation to other notes in the melody).

Examples Of Sonny's Style

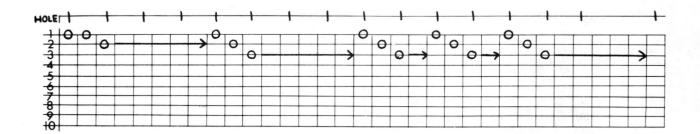

This is the opening line to *Taps*. All the notes are played on the draw (**O**) reeds. Notice the long sustained notes indicated by arrows. If you tap your foot in time to the melody (accent marks above columns), one beat should equal two columns. *Always keep time with your foot when playing the harp.*

Chugging

The first and most basic thing to learn of Sonny's is his chord rhythms, or what we can call *chugging*. Listen to the first excerpt on side one of the instruction record. Try to get the sound of the harp in your head.

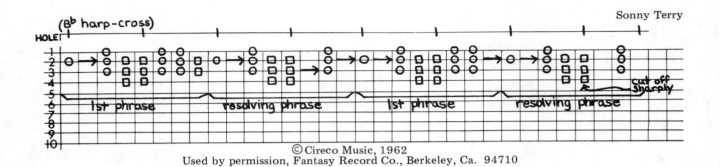

This is the opening of Sonny's *Hooray, Hooray*. More than one symbol in a column represents a chord, and again, the arrows indicate a sustain. Notice the general percussiveness of the harp. Sonny's using several techniques of percussion in this riff. Sometimes he pops his throat to accent a draw chord. Other times he uses his tongue to punctuate the draw chord by clicking off the roof of his mouth (just behind the front teeth). The single note on the #2 draw is accented in yet another way. Each time he returns to the #2 draw, his lips catch just a whisper of the #1-2-3 chord before he locks down and firmly singles out the note. This produces a little beat each time the hole is played.

In addition, of course, Sonny makes heavy use of the diaphragm in accenting the blow chords and in amplifying the effect of the other percussive techniques. The use of the diaphragm takes a long time to perfect. The more you play, the stronger and more responsive this muscle will become.

Another thing that characterizes the sound here is the way Sonny's chords, (especially the blow chord), ring out so crisp and clear. In playing chords, it is of the utmost importance to distribute your wind and pressure evenly over all the holes of the chord. Too much wind in one hole can make that reed sound slightly flat, and totally louse up the harmony of the chord. Try to *keep your lips resting softly* on the harp when playing chords that you want to ring out. As you blow or draw, *allow air to escape (or enter) from the corners of your mouth*, and whisper across the harp into the holes of the chord. Sometimes it's very useful to breathe through the nose while playing chords. This prevents an excess of pressure (and it doesn't take much) from ruining the natural resonance of the chords.

As you are playing along, remember to tap your foot on the accented beat (marks above columns). Music is time, and to be successful, you must keep good time.

Notice how the riff is in two parts. The first statement lasts through the first and second beats. The resolving statement starts on the third and lasts through the fourth beat. This resolution is almost exactly like the first phrase except that Sonny sustains the blow chord at the end, instead of breaking it into separate beats. These two complimentary phrases are then repeated over and over.

My Baby Leavin'
(On the Road/Folkways FA2369)

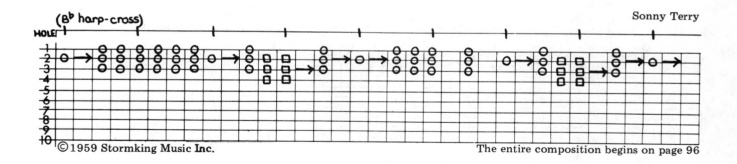

Sonny Terry

The entire composition begins on page 96

We can see this same type of resolving riff in another slightly different chord pattern that Sonny 'blows' on *My Baby Leavin'*, which can be found on side two of the instruction record.

Sonny's nephew, J. C. Burris, is playing harp along with him on this one, so it may be difficult to hear just what's happening. J. C. is doing a simple single note riff:

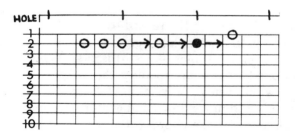

But listen to what Sonny's playing. It's the same basic chugging riff of *Hooray*, except there's more tongue clicking for those added beats. The hands are used to accent the chords on the downbeat (marks above the columns). By smacking against the harp with the free hand, while clicking the tongue off the pallate, a more forceful beat is produced. Sonny does some beautiful wails on the #3 and #4 holes (draw) to introduce the song. Once he gets into the chugging, you can hear the same resolving pattern as before. The last blow chord in the resolving part of the riff is always sustained.

As you play along with record and tab, it can be very helpful to slow things down at first. If your phonograph has a slower speed (16), give it a try. The key of the music stays about the same, and you can hear a lot more of what's happening. Or, better yet, get hold of a variable speed phonograph. Many records tend to play out of tune with the harp, which makes it hard to get the feeling when playing along. With a variable speed machine, you can tune the record to your harp.

Lost John
(Archive of Folk Music FS-206)

Sonny Terry

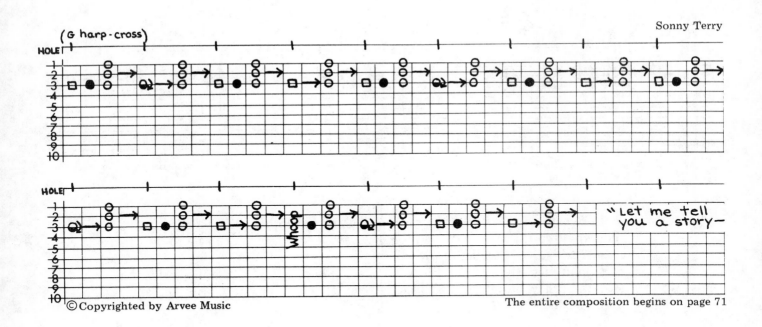

The entire composition begins on page 71

Refer again to side two of the record for *Lost John*. This song shows us a different chugging pattern, which is a good example of the beauty of chord resonance. The draw chord (holes #1—#3) is sustained on the upbeat using the attack mentioned earlier of opening the corners of the mouth, and distributing your wind evenly. As you move from the #3 hole blow to the draw chord, remember to move down and center your mouth on the #2 hole position in preparation for the chord (otherwise you'll be playing more of #2 and #3, and perhaps even a bit of #4).

This riff sounds much harder than it is to learn. The general in-out pattern makes it easier to sustain your wind over a long period of time. While the other riffs we just considered require more diaphragm, this pattern relies more on the facility for movement between the #2 and #3 holes. First, practice just this portion of the riff:

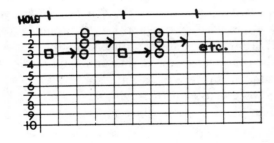

Then, try the other parts with the bend and the slide. These bend and slide notes produce a nice effect as you move them to the #2 hole position for the chord. The pressure from them gives a little snap to the draw chord. This serves the same purpose as the throat-pop in the simpler riff fragment shown above.

Once you've got these *slip* notes (pressure of #3 bend and #3 slide slipping over to the #1-2-3 chord) down well, try doing the whoop that Sonny does. It's very easy once you've got the in-out breath pattern together. Instead of blowing on the #3 hole, let out with a falsetto slip (pressure pops as you jump up to falsetto from normal). This gets rid of the air and prepares you for the #3 hole bend. Whoopin' can be a great deal of fun and certainly sounds harder than it is. (Some whoopin' Sonny does is more complex, involving in-whoops as well as out).

The importance of chord rhythms (chugging) in Sonny's playing cannot be overemphasized. They are the backbone of his style, and everything else he does flows out of them. Without playing chords, he certainly would never have become so successful as a solo performer. (Sonny presently performs with Brownie McGhee, his partner for over thirty years, but has performed solo many times). His windy, resonant attack on rhythm is hard to get, for sure. What follows may be easier to get a feel for. But, the most fundamental aspect of Sonny Terry's style is his chord work. If you can get it down well, everything else you learn from him will be influenced by it.

Intro Lines

Besides rhythm, Sonny of course plays incredible single-note lines. Here, as before, there are common elements that run through much of his single-note work. Many times we can hear the same riff repeated almost exactly from one song to another. While the similarity is important to notice, even more important is the way Sonny changes his riffs in sometimes subtle ways from song to song. He is, like many other blues people, a performer who rarely, if ever, plays a piece the same way twice. He is constantly improvising his approach to a song as he grows with the music. Taking a comparative approach, let's look at some riffs Sonny makes use of to introduce his songs. The first number we'll examine is *I Got My Eyes On You*, which is found on Side II of the instruction record.

55

I Got My Eyes On You
(Sugar Hill/Fantasy 8091)

Sonny Terry

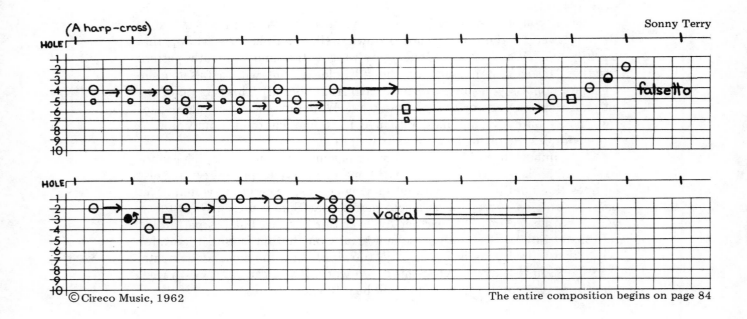

The entire composition begins on page 84

Try to follow along by reading the tab. Be sure to notice the accent marks which indicate the downbeat and the three-notes-per-beat pattern (triplet form). And always beat your foot!

Through the first eight beats (up through the blow on 6-7) Sonny is using a very thin, shrill tone (unlike many harpmen, he makes use of a variety of tone attacks, both thin and fat). Here his mouth is collapsed with the tongue lying just behind the front teeth. This leaves little space in his mouth for a deep, resonant tone. Thus, he gets that thin, piercing sound. You can use either tongue-clicks or throat-pops to achieve the beats of the draw notes here.

Now we come to an important element of Sonny's sound. See in the tab how some of the symbols used to represent chords are smaller than those above them? What this means is that you are to let one hole predominate (large symbol) over the other in playing what we might call these "favored" chords. Listen to Sonny do it again and dig the tremendous resonance of these chords. He gets just a whisper of the 5 draw along with the louder 4 draw. The 6 and 7 blow is an incredible sound, and here he gets perhaps a little more of the subordinant hole.

Be careful not to get too much of the understated note in there. You'll ruin the melody completely. You could actually play the line with just the single notes (the larger symbols—these really carry the melody, the subordinant holes add texture). But we're after the whole of Sonny's sound, not just the melody, right?

After the long sustain on the 6-7 blow, Sonny plays a nice riff coming down to the 2 hole. Notice the clarity in the way he singles out each hole. Here he retires to a mellower full tone (try opening the mouth cavity for more resonance), rather than staying shrill and biting. Practice just this portion of the line by itself. Try to get each hole clear and the timing just right. (Keep that foot going!)

Following the falsetto voice, Sonny plays a little riff he uses in many places as a *ride* (a line that's used in the spaces between the lyrics to accent the vocal message). There are several other rides we'll deal with later. But, right here, a good thing to get down and spend some time on in this riff is the slide inflection:

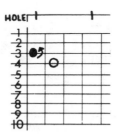

Listen to Sonny do it again. See how fluid it can sound. The key to it is in the emphasis of the slide note as a punctuation (downbeat) and the 4 draw as a lighter afternote. The movement from 3 to 4 must coordinate with the end of the slide, and the heavy pressure from the slide must be gone when you reach 4 draw. Otherwise, you'll bend the 4 note. Spend some time with it and try to build your own riffs using this little fragment. Sonny makes many riffs with this thing.

Easy Rider
(Folkways, FA 2369)

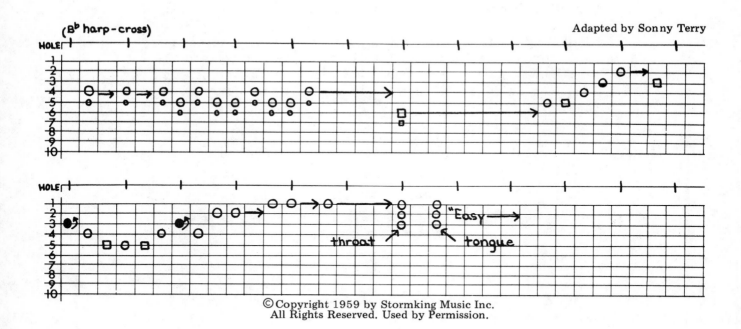

(B♭ harp-cross)

Adapted by Sonny Terry

throat

"Easy

tongue

Listen to the second cut on side one of the instruction record. This intro is very similar to what we just heard. Again, it's in triplet form. It has the same basic melodic line, with the use, once more, of favored, resonating two-note chords.

But notice how Sonny changes the opening part a little, *swinging* between those 4-5 and 5-6 chords in a more rhythmic way (faintly reminiscent of John Lee "Sonny Boy" Williamson). After the comedown from 6-7 blow, here he chooses to play a line rather than sing the falsetto as before.

Try to get a feeling for this up and down type of pattern. The up complements the down phrase. Practice this by itself many times. The key to it is in that little slide from the 3 draw that we just dealt with. Get the notes singled out clearly and work on the timing. Be careful about that 5 draw. Keep a mellow attack on it. It's very easy to bend it flat.

Finally, listen to the last two chord beats Sonny blows, just before the vocal comes in. In playing this chord (1-2-3), remember to have your mouth centered over the #2 hole position. The first beat is a throat-pop with the tongue laying loose. (It helps to drop your jaw a bit for this at first). As the throat contracts for the beat, it pulls the tongue up to the roof of the mouth. Then click your tongue off the palate, while closing your jaw for the second beat. Sustain the chord after the tongue click and let those reeds ring out by letting the air in from the corners of your mouth. This type of chord beating can be heard in a lot of Sonny's songs as a fill or ride between the lyrics.

Blues All Around My Bed
(Folkways FA2369)

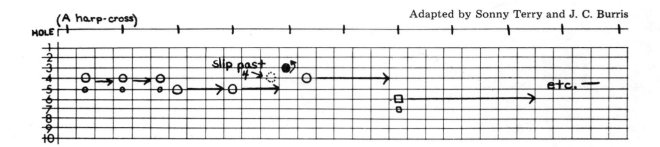

Let's take a look at this one more intro (you'll find it on side one, cut #3 of the instruction record), which again sounds quite similar to the others. But while the first two seemed to have almost a bugle call, *Reveille* quality, this intro is slower and more mournful, like a New Orleans funeral march song.

Focus on just one thing Sonny's doing here, which illustrates another technique of percussion. Listen several times to this cut and see if you hear that little slip effect as Sonny comes down to the slide on #3. Instead of just moving down and then drawing in again for the #3 slide, he keeps breathing in while he slips quickly past the 4 hole. As he arrives at the #3, he's already developed the pressure for the bend and you hear kind of a snap as the reed explodes into the slide. This is similar to what we heard on *Lost John* as he slipped from #3 bend to 1-2-3 chord. Here, though, he's slipping into a bend rather than out of one.

As he moves from the slide on #3 to the 4 hole, remember that *all the pressure from the bend is gone* when he plays the mellower 4 draw. This modulation from high pressure to low pressure, open-throat breathing (or vice-versa) is an important element of all blues harp. We'll hear it again in some other things Sonny does.

Ride Phrases

The next six selections we'll consider exemplify what I've described earlier as *rides* or *fills*. These riffs are played in between the parts of the vocal line and function to accent the flow of feeling that the lyrics describe. In many ways, they are similar to the intro lines and may be used as such, or as parts of *turnaround* phrases, which we'll cover later. While there is much in common among all the riffs on the record and in the tap, their function as they appear in different parts of the progression is important for you to consider.

59

Mean Old Woman
(Robbin' The Grave, BL 101)

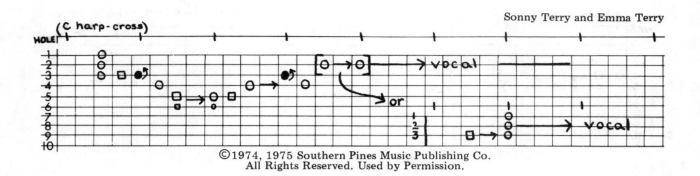

Sonny Terry and Emma Terry

Refer to side one for this next cut. This is one of Sonny's most recent songs. The ride here is the same riff we heard in *Easy Rider*, but Sonny's changed the pattern of the rhythm. Instead of the triplet form, here we have a jumpier four-notes-to-the-beat rhythm. Notice how the notes on the downbeat are more heavily accented than they were in the *Easy Rider* intro. While *Easy Rider* was smoother and mellower, emphasizing the richness of single notes, *Mean Old Woman* is more stark, with a shriller, favored-chord attack (large versus small symbols).

The tab here shows two similar riffs, but their endings differ. See if you can hear where Sonny is blowing on 3 rather than drawing on 2. It makes no difference which way you prefer to do it. The main thing to understand is the advantage of having a draw reed (#2) and a blow reed(#3) adjacent to each other that both sound the same note. We saw in *Lost John* how this can be a real help in conserving your wind. If your lungs are getting full, you may choose to blow on the 3. If they are getting empty, you may wish to draw on the 2 hole.

You can hear the same thing at work in the beginning of the ride just before the slide note. Here Sonny clicks his tongue for the draw chord and then plays blow 3. He might have chosen to play draw 2 instead, but his lungs were prepared for a blow. This alternate in-out attack, made effective by the action of the diaphragm, gives more jumpiness to the whole riff.

Poor Man But A Good Man
(Folkways FA2369)

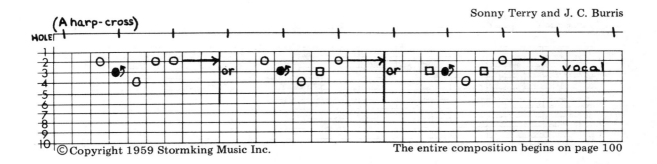

Sonny Terry and J. C. Burris

(A harp- cross)

The entire composition begins on page 100

In *Poor Man*, (side two) we can hear the same basic slide 3, draw 4 motif that Sonny makes use of so often. You can see how important it is to get this little tool down. The ride Sonny plays on this cut is a good context in which to practice this slide. Despite the simplicity of the harp here, it is beautifully self-sufficient in accenting the vocal. The bones really aren't essential to the feeling at all. This is Sonny at his most concise level of expression. You can see that the harp doesn't have to be flashy and complicated to be enough.

Poor Man offers a good example of another reason why Sonny sometimes chooses to blow on the #3, rather than draw on 2. Notice in the tab the three ways I have charted the ride phrase here. The three describe varying degrees of the use of blow 3. The first way describes the riff with all draw notes. The second has one blow 3 note and the third has two blow notes. Make your own choice as to which sounds best. But you have to understand this one more advantage of blow 3.

Blowing on 3 before the slide on 3 sets your diaphragm up for the best attack on that slide note. Since you need more pressure, more *pull* in order to bend or slide a note, your diaphragm has to be ready to give you that pull. If you have just played draw 2, your diaphragm is out of its best position for the attack on the slide. Depending on the strength and development of your diaphragm, you can execute the slide attack either way. But in terms of efficiency and smoothness, blow 3 is a better choice.

At the end of this ride, you have the same option of blowing or drawing, and either sounds good. Sonny is blowing on 3, and in a sense, this sets him up for either a draw 2 or the draw chord. The position of the diaphragm is not so critical here, as there is no bend or slide to worry about.

As Sonny concludes the verse, he plays a riff followed by the ride phrase again, just as he goes to the turnaround. Try to get a feel for the way these two parts go together. The second part (ride) *completes* the first. This type of complementary action is going on in much of Sonny's music. We can hear it again in the next piece.

Sweet Woman Blues
(Fantasy 8091)

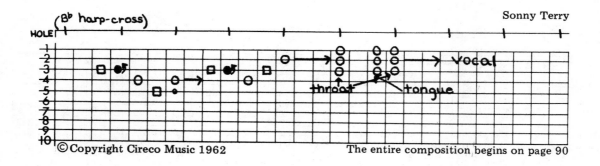

          The entire composition begins on page 90

In *Sweet Woman* Sonny combines short ride riffs to produce a single extended ride phrase, in the spaces between the vocal lines, which in this case are longer. The first part of the ride, once again, has that slide up on the three hold. Be sure to notice the resonance of that favored 4-5 chord at the end of the first riff. The second riff in this extended ride is the *Poor Man* we looked at before. Listen to the way these two parts go together, the first (which ends on the 4-5 holes) being completed by the second (which ends on the 2 hole-tonic).

Sonny even has room for a third part in this ride phrase. He adds some chord beats here that we heard before in *Easy Rider*. Try using the technique I described earlier of throat versus tongue on these chords. If you have real trouble with this (the throat, like the diaphragm, takes a lot of practice to become responsive) try playing the following instead:

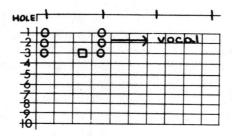

Use tongue clicks for the draw chords and blow on 3. This approximates the same rhythm as playing all draw. Make a real effort, however, to get the throat technique down. Its development will coincide with that of the diaphragm. So, be patient and keep practicing.

I Got A Little Girl
(Fantasy 8091)

Sonny Terry

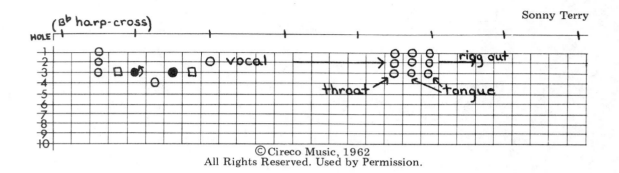

Listen to the next cut on side one. This song is a good example of how chugging in itself can be used as a ride between the lyrics. It also demonstrates, once again, how Sonny takes a riff and changes it around slightly to fit into a different framework.

In this cut, Sonny's using something like the ride you heard in *Poor Man*, but he's changed the rhythm around (from triplet form to four notes per beat) and added some notes. After he plays the slide #3, draw 4, he goes to the bend on 3 rather than the blow 3 as in *Poor Man*. Try this move a number of times. It's a bit tricky until you have some facility with your throat and diaphragm. Because of the move from draw to draw-bend, your diaphragm is not ideally set up for the pull on 3 bend as it was for the slide.

After the bend on 3, Sonny blows 3 and draws on 2, and here again we can see the advantage of having the same two notes on either a blow or a draw. The out-in effect of the diaphragm produces a better rhythm attack than would the tongue or throat if the riff were played:

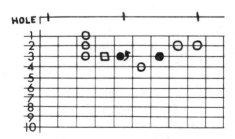

Try it like this a few times. It just doesn't have the same smoothness. And since you're playing five draw notes in a row, those last two probably won't sound as strong as they could.

Try using the ride in this cut along with the chugging we heard Sonny do on *Hooray, Hooray*. They work well together. As you learn more and more of Sonny's licks, it's a good idea to play around and put them together in your own way. By doing this, you'll develop more of a feel for the style in general. And you'll have more fun!

63

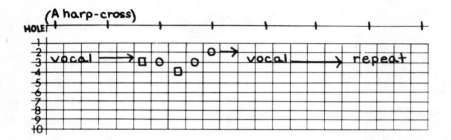

This ride is perhaps the most fundamental riff we've considered so far. It doesn't require a bend note, slide note, or chord. Just simple, clean, single notes. But the riff may be harder to get than you think.

While bends and slides may be more difficult for you to master, playing clean, natural tones is not that much easier. All depend on the development of the throat muscles and diaphragm. In bending, you learn to contract your throat. In sliding, you learn to contract or expand your throat in a variable manner. In playing the natural tones in the riff, you have to keep your throat open and breathe more deeply from the diaphragm. This takes a lot of practice, but once you feel your throat muscles starting to do things, you'll know you're on the right track. As your diaphragm gets stronger and more under your control, everything you play including open-throat things, will sound better.

Another very fundamental thing the ride shows here is the importance of singling out holes neatly. Remember that a sloppy attempt at singling out holes can result in a slight unintended bend (especially on #2 and #3 draw). If you purse your lips too much over the hole, you'll have this trouble. But if you relax your lips (let the harp sink into them a bit) and concentrate on the corners of your mouth, your singling technique and adeptness at movement from one hole to another will be greatly improved. Don't be discouraged if you can't get this technique down, even after sustained effort. As I mentioned before, all your tools develop concurrently, and each influences the facility of the other.

Turnarounds

A turnaround, as described earlier, is that portion of a verse just at the very end of the progression. It functions as both a concluding phrase and as a sort of preparation for the next verse. So, it can be viewed as an introduction. In fact, an intro line is essentially nothing but a turnaround placed just before the first verse of a song. To view any particular riff Sonny plays as necessarily an intro, a ride, or a turnaround, is really just an arbitrary matter. I have chosen to do this primarily to provide a context in which to examine the mechanics of playing. But it is important to understand the functional aspects of how and why a riff is used in a certain place.

Your body has five parts (muscle groups) that you can work with in playing harp; the hands, the lips, the tongue, the throat, and the diaphragm. There are countless ways in which you can combine these tools to produce sounds on the harp. I've talked about all of these things to some extent (the hands will be covered in more depth later), but I'd like to focus more specifically now on just the throat and its use in playing an important riff Sonny uses many times as a turnaround.

Keep On Walkin'
(Fantasy 8091)

Brownie McGhee

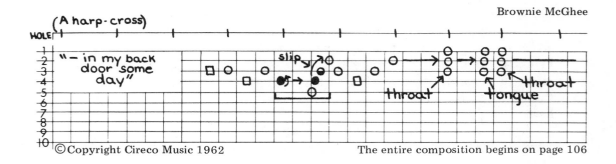

          The entire composition begins on page 106

Find *Keep On Walkin'* on side two of the instruction record. First, as before, just listen to this piece several times through, paying close attention to the turnaround riff that Sonny blows. It's a good idea to slow your machine down for the riff, if you've got a slower speed. If not, you can tape it on any standard recorder and play it back at one of the slower speeds most of these machines include. This is a very tough move to learn, and it's really almost impossible to hear what's happening without slowing it down.

As I mentioned before, the throat is most important in this riff. Now, by the throat, I'm referring to the muscles that line the throat, expanding and contracting to produce the slides and bends. These muscles extend from the back of the mouth, down to where your esophagus meets your windpipe. In fact, the tongue is actually one of these muscles. It, too, extends back and becomes the lower part of your throat cavity. It's a bit confusing then, to speak of throat constriction (choking) as opposed to lip or tongue constriction (squeezing) when actually there are several places back in your throat where the constriction can take place.

Many harp players drop their jaws and pull their tongues back to constrict for the bends and slides. This action brings the back of the tongue up against the end of the palate, just at the throat opening. This technique requires considerable pull from the diaphragm. Sonny's technique is to constrict the muscles which line the *back* of the throat. His tongue doesn't move and his jaw doesn't drop. These muscles are able to constrict the air flow to a greater extent than the tongue and palate technique. Thus, Sonny doesn't have to pull as hard on the diaphragm in order to get the bend or slide notes.

If you're used to the first technique, Sonny's method may be elusive. Concentrate on the sound of Sonny's slide down from the 4 hole. Try to compare him to anyone else whom you've heard play this inflection. There are several different tone qualities you can get in this slide depending on the point of constriction within your mouth and throat. Experiment with this slide as much as you can. Your muscles have to learn the right feel, and this takes time. Listen to Sonny play this turnaround as many times as it takes for you to *get the sound in your head.*

While Sonny's choking technique is foremost in learning this turnaround riff, the way in which it is combined with the precision of movement from hole to hole is important to understand. Consider for now, just the bracketed portion of the tab. Notice the movement from the 4 hole to the 5 hole and back to the 4 hole again. As you go to the 5 hole, your throat has opened up from the action of the slide on 4. But as you move back to 4, you must have your throat constricted once again for the bend, *precisely as you arrive there.* Otherwise, you may be playing more of a slide than just the bend. As you slip down from 4 to 2, you get that snapping action I talked about in *Blues All Around My Bed* and *Lost John.* The pressure from your throat on #4 bend causes the #3 and #2 holes to pop as you move down the harp.

This combination of throat constriction and precise timing of movement is of such importance that I'd like to present two more examples of this move from the 4 hole down to the 2.

Sonny and Brownie in Harlem, 1959.

Cold Wind Blowin'
(Robbin' the Grave LP)

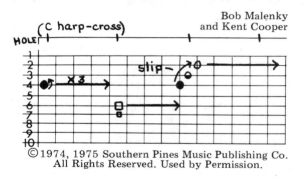

Bob Malenky
and Kent Cooper

In this selection (side one, cut seven) you can hear the great facility Sonny has for synchronizing his choking with the movement of his lips across the harp. The preceding turnaround riff showed us a movement between adjacent holes. Here Sonny moves from blow 6-7 directly to the bend on 4. His lips and hands know just where that 4 hole is. Practice this move many times. Your body will learn to feel the distance between these holes, too. After this move, we hear the same snapping slip down from 4 that Sonny played on the last cut. It stands out more emphatically here, and this is a good cut to practice with.

Baby, I Knocked On Your Door
(Fantasy 8091)

Sonny Terry

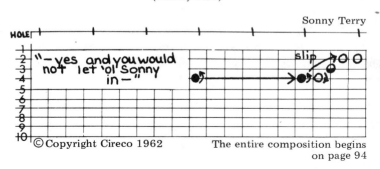

   The entire composition begins on page 94

Listen to the next cut on side one very closely. Besides the same slip down from the 4 bend, it contains a slide inflection we haven't heard yet. Pay attention to the tab symbols which indicate a slide up and then a slide down on the 4 draw (marked in bracket). These slides flow into each other in a smooth, uninterrupted manner. Listen to the riff again and notice the short space of time in which all these notes occur. At first, it will be difficult to play the riff this smoothly. Slow down your record machine and practice along. At this speed, it's easier to get those slides to flow together nicely.

These last three numbers I discussed should be considered together. They all illustrate Sonny's unique way of choking the 4 hole, and the importance of synchronizing the action of the throat muscles with the movement of the lips across the harp. In practicing these riffs, (or any others), try to break things down into component parts as I've done in the text. Try playing just portions of the riff at a time, until you get them down. Then put them together. You'll be surprised how much better the whole thing sounds.

Special Effects

As I've mentioned before, there are great limitations to the use of any form of tablature. Reading through a tab will teach you nothing, if you don't spend much time listening and practicing. It's your body that learns to make music, and not your mind. The tab system in this book is just an aid to you in locating on the harp the various kinds of notes you hear played on the record, and in organizing them in a framework of time. It does not show you what the notes sound like.

I'd like to take a little time here to demonstrate some things that Sonny does, some kinds of special effects. Since they involve no movement on the harp there's no need for a tab of them.

Trills

The first special effect is a *trill*, a fast, alternating movement between two holes on the harp. Most harp players do this by shaking their head or by moving the harp. Sonny trills by wiggling his tongue back and forth between the two holes.

Flutters

Fluttering is another special effect Sonny uses. He beats his tongue on and off the palate very quickly while breathing in. Each time he goes on or off the palate an accent is produced. Let's listen to Sonny do it on *Baby, I Knocked On Your Door* (Sugar Hill/Fantasy 8091). He's using an A harp.

Throat Pops

Throat pops sound similar to flutters. But it's the throat contracting and expanding very quickly that gives you the accents here. I can't do it nearly as fast as Sonny, but it sounds something like this number he calls *Playing With the Thing* (Robbin' the Grave/Blue Labor BL-101). Sonny's playing an A harp.

The last thing I want to consider here is the way Sonny uses his hands. Of course, Sonny uses them to amplify the other techniques I've mentioned throughout the book. Here, though, I want to show you three special things that Sonny does with his hands.

The Hand Smack

The first is a *hand smack*. While holding the harp in one hand, you smack your free hand against the palm of your holding hand. At the same time, breathe in and try playing a slide on the #4 hole.

The Wah-Wah Effect and Fanning the Harp

The last two techniques are the *wah-wah* effect and *fanning the harp*. For the wah-wahs, start with your hands tightly cupped around the harp. Then breathe in while opening your cup by sort of pivoting from the palms or wrist area.

To fan the harp, start with your hands cupped around the harp again. But this time open and close your cup much faster. Your free hand can either pivot on the holding hand or you can fan it back and forth, each time completely losing contact with the holding hand. Listen to the last cut of Sonny here. See if you can hear where he's fanning and where he makes the wah-wah sound. This is from the *Jailhouse Blues* (On the Road/Folkways FA 2369). Sonny's using a B♭ harp.

The Songs

On the following pages you'll find sixteen of Sonny Terry's best-known songs, written in the harp notation used in the previous section. Several of these songs appear on side two of the instruction record and it is important that you listen as you make use of the tab. As I've said before, the fundamental thing is the sound. Tablature, by itself, is of little use to anyone. For those songs which do not appear on the record, refer to the discography.

To conserve space, two new symbols have been added to the tablature in this section. For long sustains on notes and chords a simple X 1, X 2, X 3, etc., written over or under the sustain arrow indicates the total length of the sustain. For riffs which are repeated several times, brackets are used to indicate the riff, and the multiplication sign (X) over, under, or after the bracket, is used to show how many times the riff is repeated. In addition, chord changes and accents for guitar are shown where are applicable.

As you try playing along with Sonny on these songs, you might find it easier to hear what's happening if you slow down your record player. There's a lot of harp going on here (especially those heavy instrumentals).

I'm sure a great deal more could be written about what Sonny's doing, his style and technique. But, I think there can be only so much writing and talking about harp. The rest has to be listening and playing. It's the only way to learn.

So lay back in there and dig the master. And start digging yourself, too.

Lost John

Sonny Terry

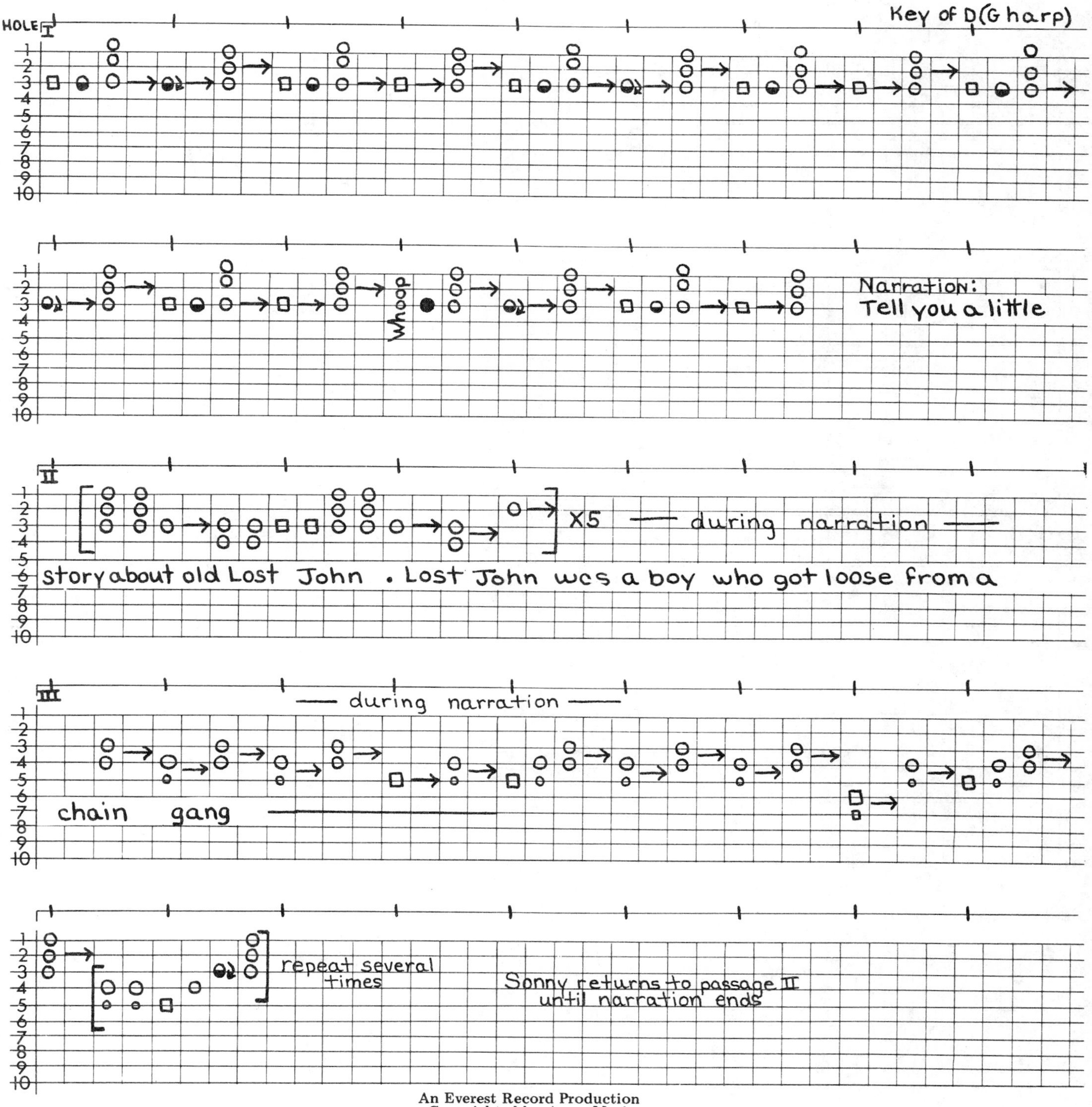

HOLE I
Key of D (G harp)
Narration:
Tell you a little
Whoop
II
X5 — during narration —
story about old Lost John. Lost John wcs a boy who got loose from a
III
— during narration —
chain gang
repeat several times
Sonny returns to passage II until narration ends

An Everest Record Production

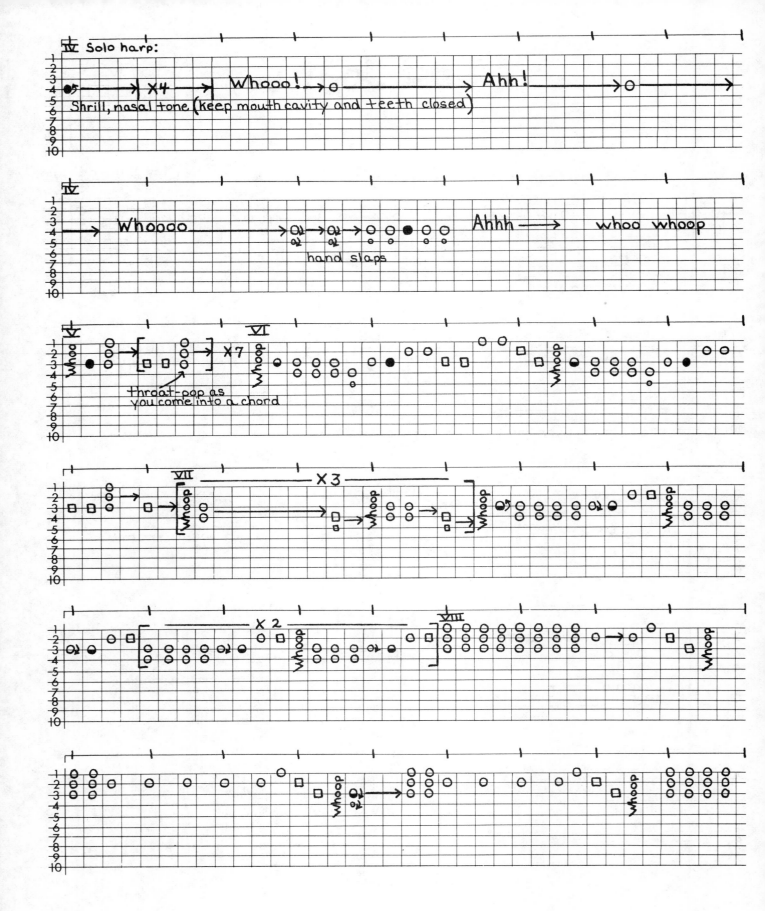

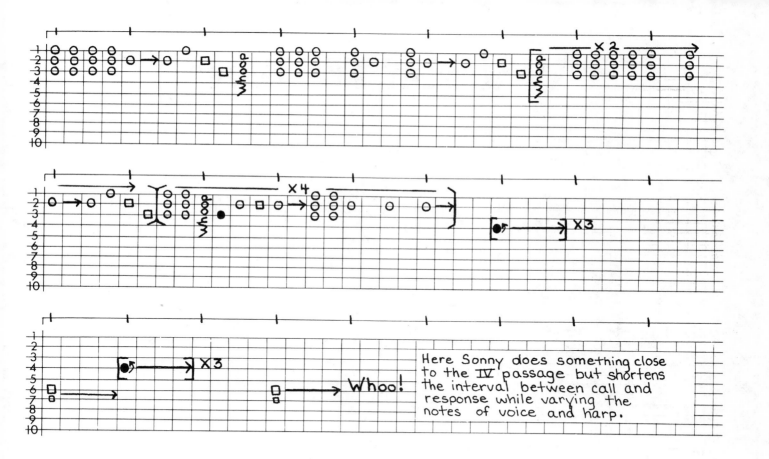

Here Sonny does something close to the IV passage but shortens the interval between call and response while varying the notes of voice and harp.

Lost John
(narrative by Woody Guthrie)

Let me tell you a little story about old Lost John. Lost John was a boy who got loose from a chain gang, down in Louisiana. 'Bout sixteen bloodhounds sniffin' after him, sheriffs, deputies and everybody else in the country chasin' him, comin' across the swamp. Lost John outrun the bloodhounds there, all night long.

Just along towards the mornin' he looked up through the trees there and seen the lights from a house. He didn't know whether the people inside was friends or enemies. So he wanted to go up to the house though and ask them if he could stay there to get away from the bloodhounds. Still he was afraid if he did go up there that the people might set their dogs around barkin' at him, or shoot him down with a Winchester rifle. Here's a story 'bout Lost John.

Whoopin' The Blues

Sonny Terry
Key of E (A harp)

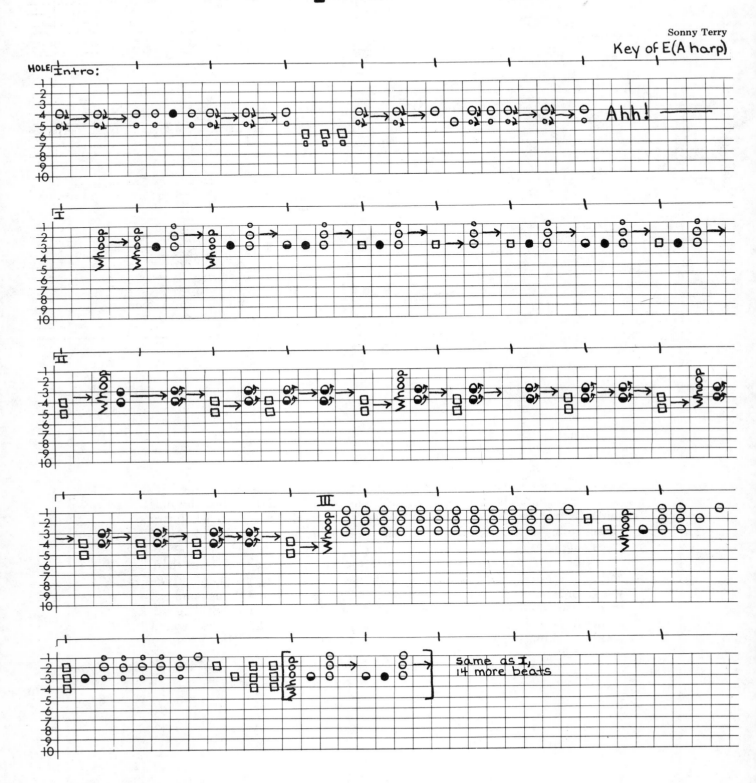

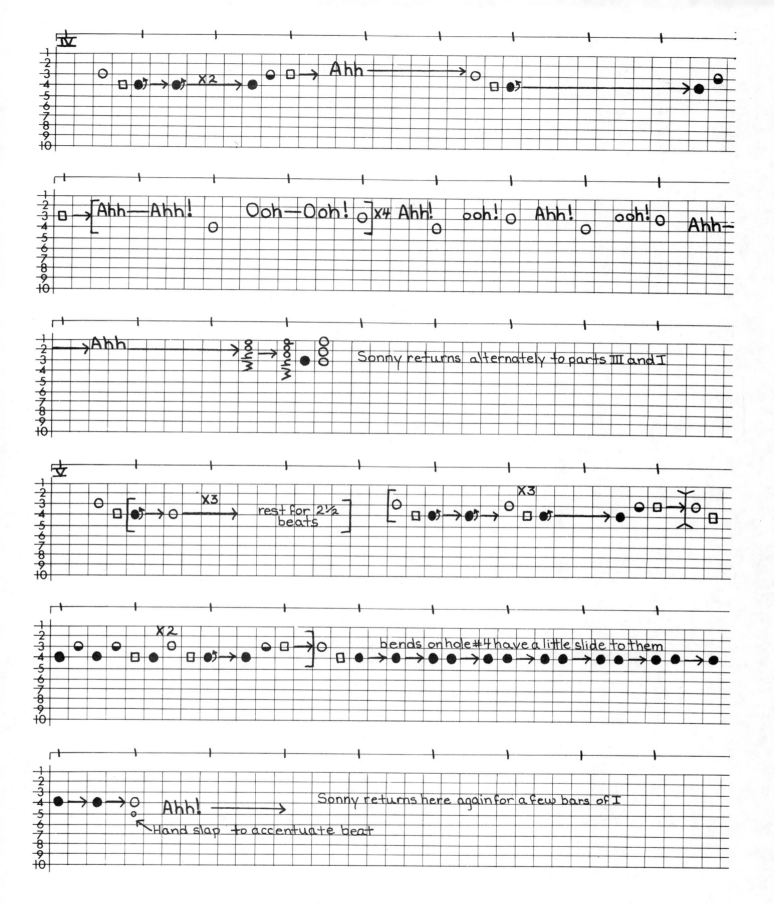

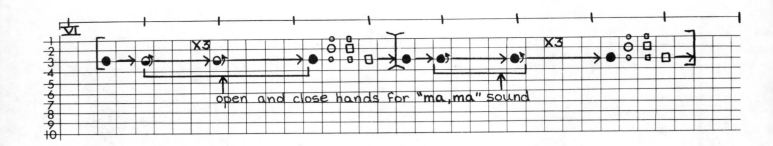

After VI Sonny alternates between harp and vocal for the "mama".
Notice the half-tone modulation (3 hole bends) on harp and guitar.
He then returns to some of passages I and III before concluding with :

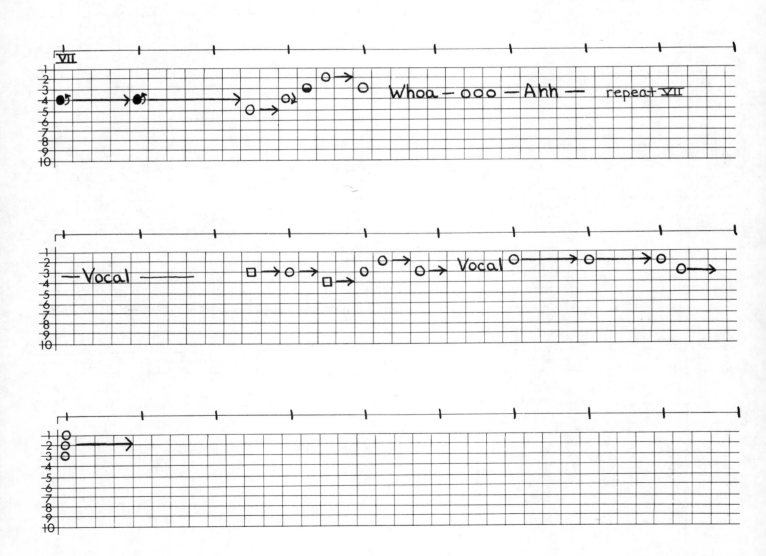

At the Apollo Theatre, 1966.

Harmonica With Slaps

Sonny Terry and J. C. Burris
Key of E (A harp)

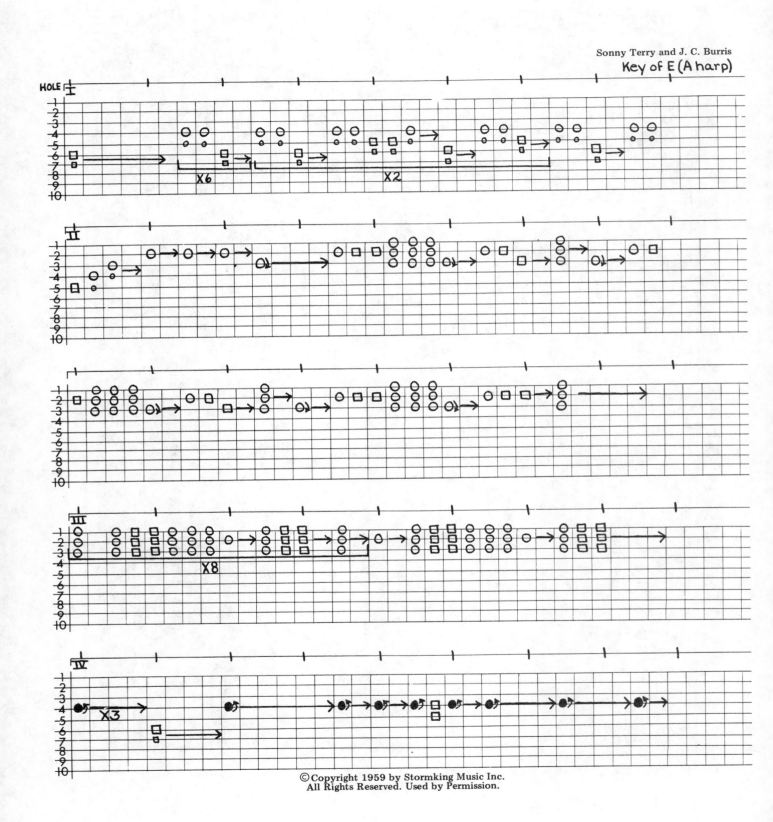

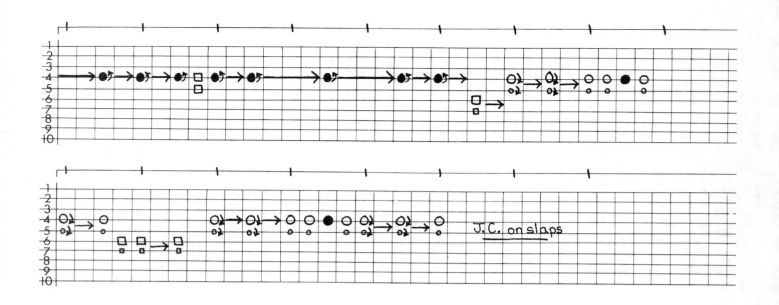

Sonny now returns to III for twenty beats, then plays twenty beats of II again, after which he goes way up on the #9 hole for this:

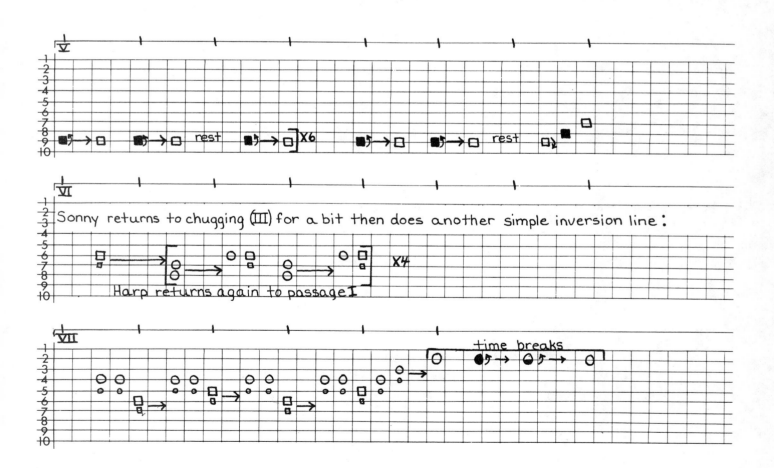

Sonny returns to chugging (III) for a bit then does another simple inversion line:

Harp returns again to passage I

Dirty Mistreater

Sonny Terry

Key of F (B♭ harp)

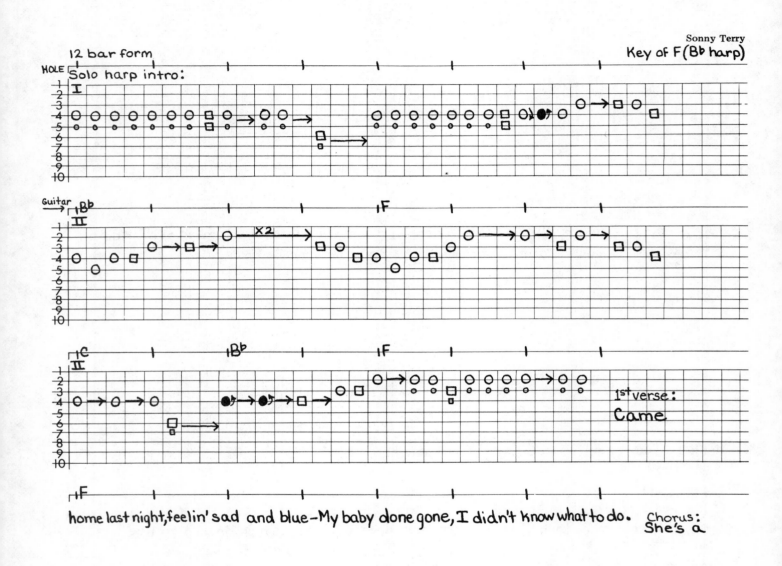

home last night, feelin' sad and blue—My baby done gone, I didn't know what to do. Chorus: She's a

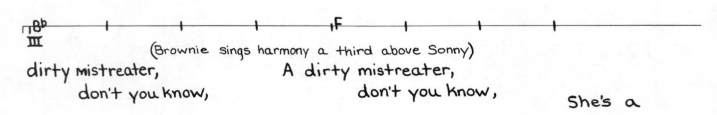

(Brownie sings harmony a third above Sonny)

dirty mistreater,   A dirty mistreater,
   don't you know,   don't you know,

                                        She's a

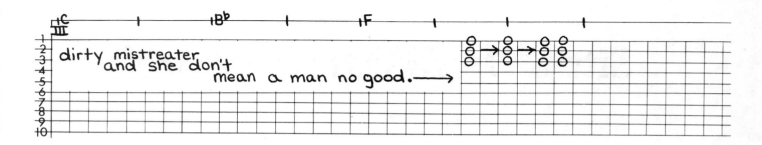

2nd Verse:

Work hard for her, every day,
She took my money and throwed it away.

Chorus: (As above in passage III)
Sonny plays <u>two progressions</u> of I and II, varying only slightly parts of I as follows:

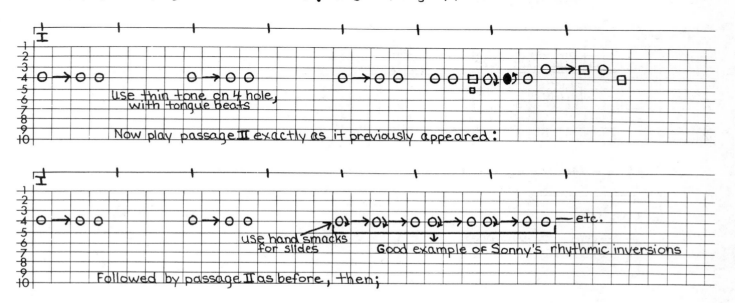

I cooked her breakfast, carried it
  to her bed,
I took my comb and combed her
  head.

Chorus:

Well, I give her my money, bought
  her fine, nice clothes,
If I find her, I bust her right in her
  nose.

Chorus:

*(Sonny plays two more progressions
of I and II as before, then;)*

I done sung this song, I didn't tell
  no lie,
The day I found her, that's the day
  she died.

Chorus:

*(Sonny repeats two more progressions
of I and II to conclude song.)*

Sittin' On Top Of The World

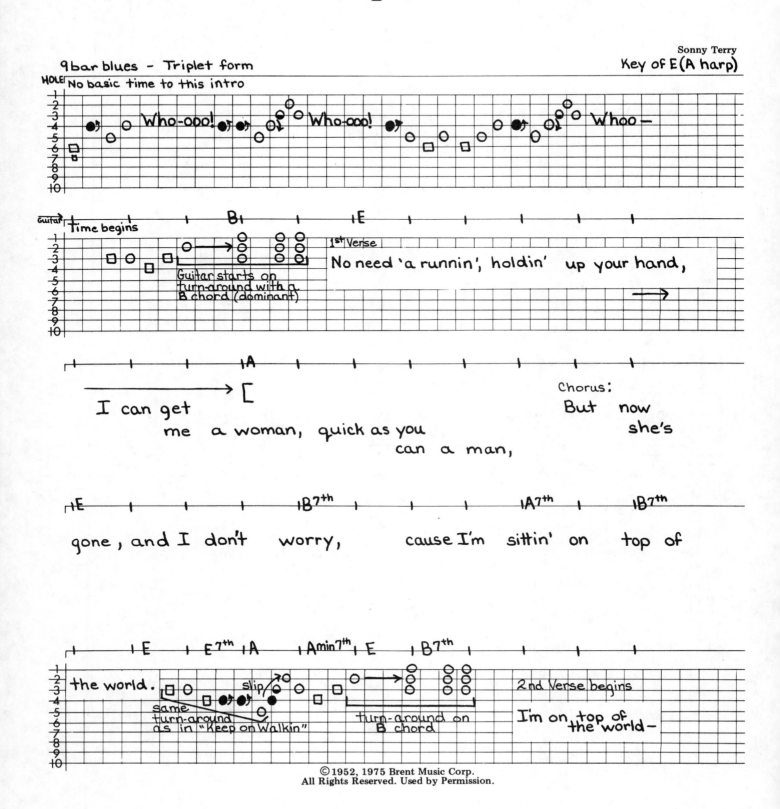

2nd Verse
I'm on top of the world, with my leg hanging down,
My baby done quit me, gone out 'a this town.

Chorus:

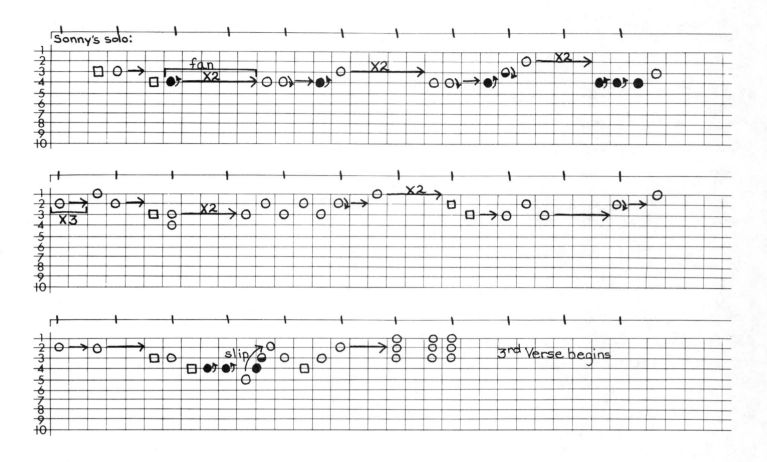

Work all the summer, and all the fall,
Now they wanna take my Christmas,
    and my overalls.

Chorus:

*(After the chorus, Sonny plays the same
turnaround phrase as before.)*

Bye, bye, baby, honey if you call it
    gone,
It may worry me some, baby, but it
    won't last long.

Chorus:

*(Sonny plays same turnaround as before,
but add the following to end song:)*

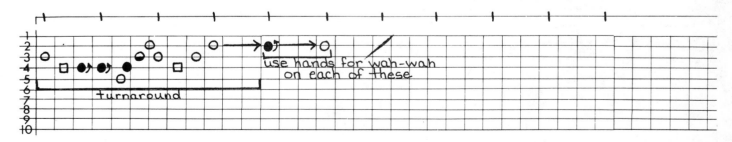

I Got My Eyes On You

Sonny Terry

Key of E (A harp)

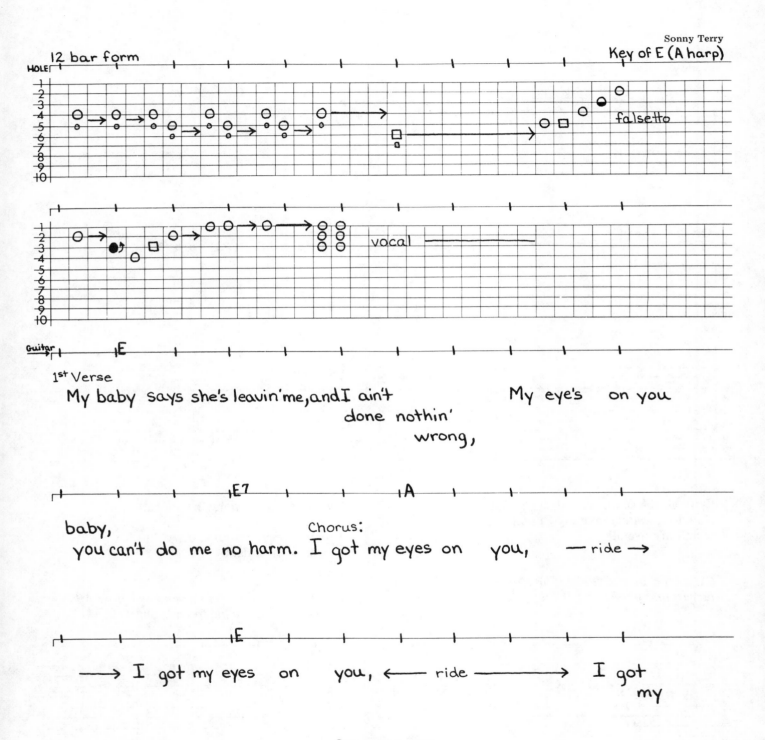

1st Verse

My baby says she's leavin' me, and I ain't done nothin' wrong, My eye's on you

baby, you can't do me no harm. Chorus: I got my eyes on you, — ride →

⟶ I got my eyes on you, ⟵ — ride ⟶ I got my

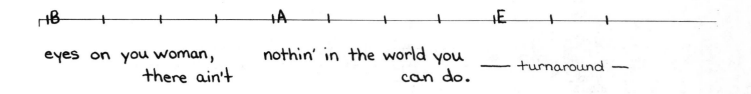

eyes on you woman,   nothin' in the world you
       there ain't   can do.   — turnaround —

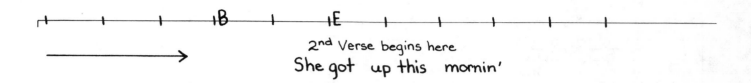

2nd Verse begins here
She got up this mornin'

2nd Verse:
She got up this mornin', whoa, 'bout the break of day,
Run to the door tryin' to make a getaway.

Chorus:

3rd Verse:
C'mon in this house little girl, and make yourself at home,
Know you can't leave me, all alone.

Chorus:

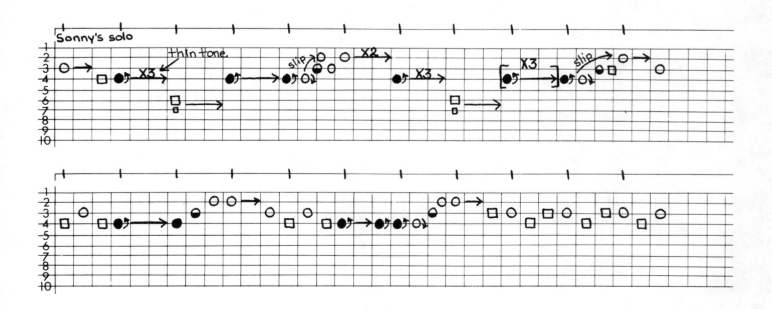

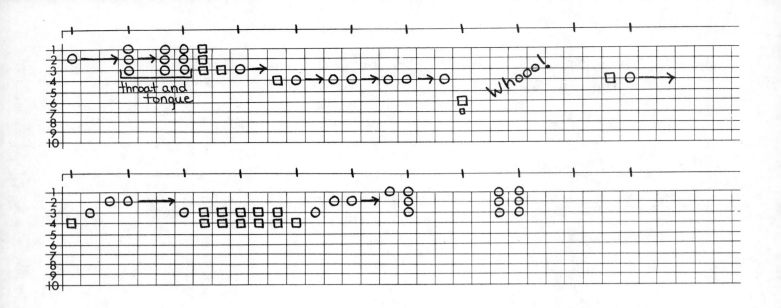

I cooked the little girl breakfast, and
   I served it in the bed,
Now she want to leave, but she heard
   what I said.

Chorus:

I gived her all my money, and I
   thought I was doin' right,
If she tempt that evil again, you
   know it's bound to be a fight.

Chorus:

I took the little girl in, people, you
   know I treated her just like a queen,
Now she want to leave, but it don't
   mean a thing.

Chorus:

Airplane Blues

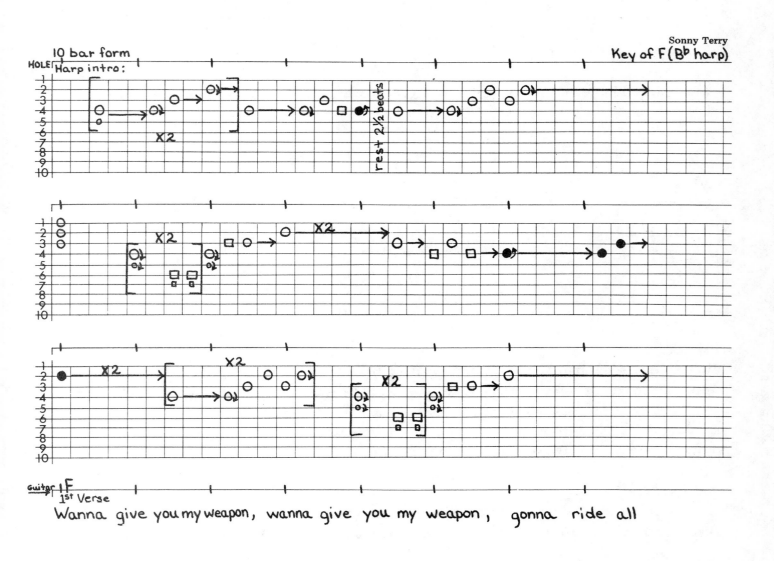

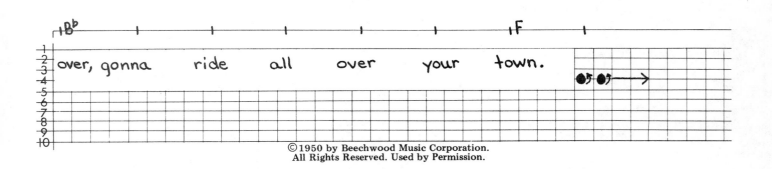

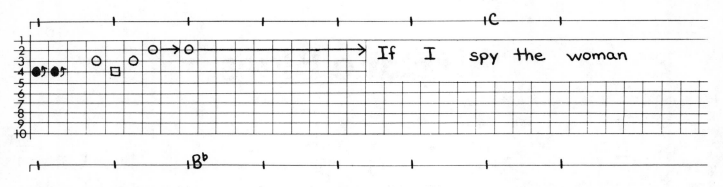

If I spy the woman

I'm lovin', I'm sure gone let my airplane, I'm sure gone let my

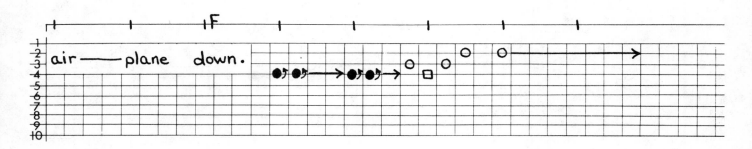

air —— plane down.

2nd Verse:
Honey here's my hand, honey here's my hand,
You can lead me where you want, you can lead me where you want me
      to go. (Harp ride same as 1st verse)
If you lead me wrong this time, then you won't lead me,
Then you won't lead me no more. (Harp ride)

3rd Verse:
Honey you three times seven, honey you three times seven,
And you know what you wanna, and you know what you wanna do. (Same
      harp ride)
Well, that day you quit me little woman, and I won't be mad,
And I won't be mad with you. (Harp ride)

Harp break – same as intro progression.

4th Verse:
I know my little woman, I know my little woman,
She's bound to jump, she's bound to jump and shout. (Harp ride)
When she gets hold to this letter, I done wrote my long time,
I done wrote my long time lost. (Harp ride)

5th Verse:
Just the day before Christmas, just the day before Christmas,
Let me bring your present, let me bring your present tonight. (Harp ride)
That will be you Santa Clause, even if my whiskers,
Even if my whiskers be white. (Harp ride)

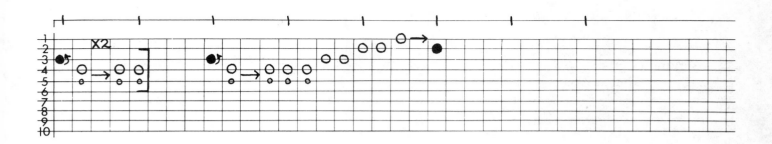

Sweet Woman Blues

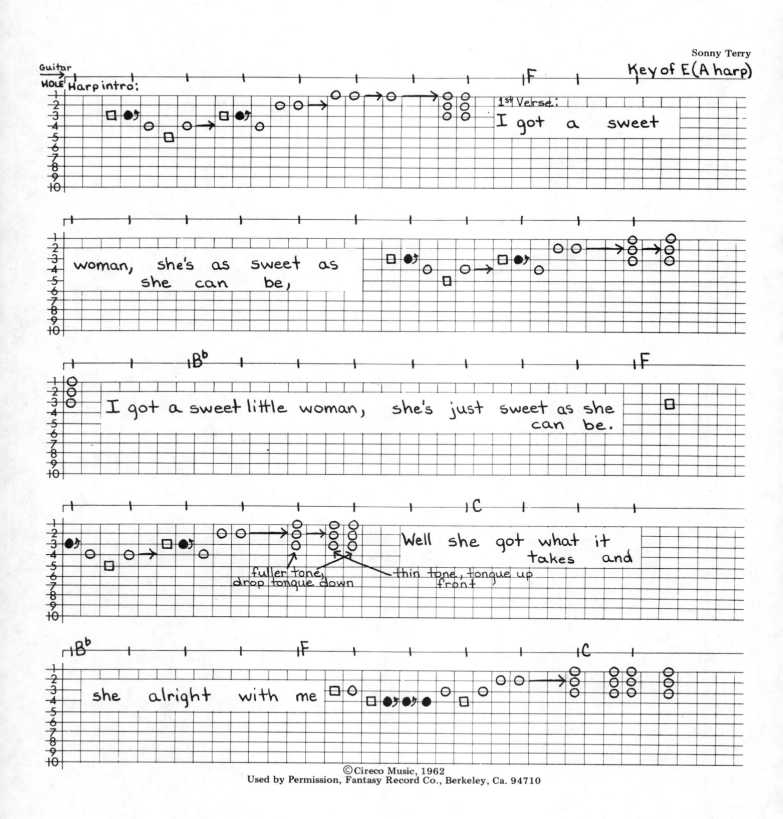

2nd Verse:
I call her my sugar, (harp ride) but sugar never was so sweet. (harp ride)
I call her my sugar, (harp ride) but sugar never was so sweet. (harp ride)
Every time I meet the little girl,
She knocks old Sonny off his feet.

3rd Verse:
Well, she's so sweet and lovin', (harp ride) I'm gonna tell it everywhere.(harp ride)
Well, she's so sweet and lovin', (harp ride) I'm gonna tell it everywhere.(harp ride)
Well she knocks old Sonny out,
The way she wears her hair.

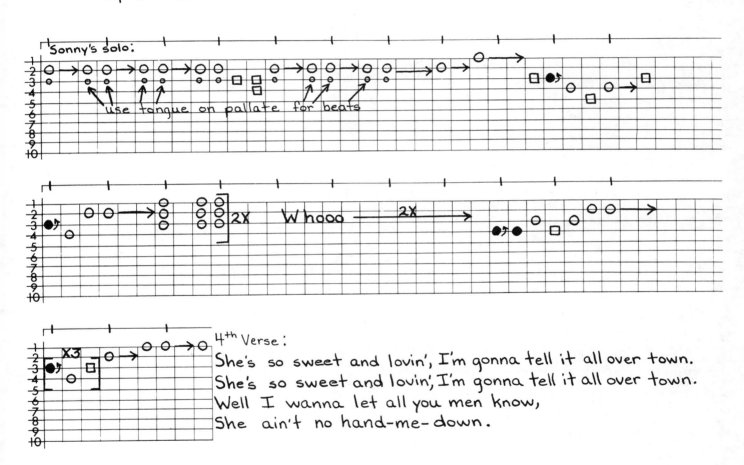

4th Verse:
She's so sweet and lovin', I'm gonna tell it all over town.
She's so sweet and lovin', I'm gonna tell it all over town.
Well I wanna let all you men know,
She ain't no hand-me-down.

5th Verse:
She's so sweet and lovin', I'm gonna tell it everywhere I go.
She's so sweet and lovin', I'm gonna tell it everywhere I go.
Well, if she ever leave me,
You know it going to hurt me so.

6th Verse :
I love that little woman and I ain't gonna tell no lie.
I love that little woman and I ain't gonna tell no lie.
Well the day she quit me,
That's the day I die.

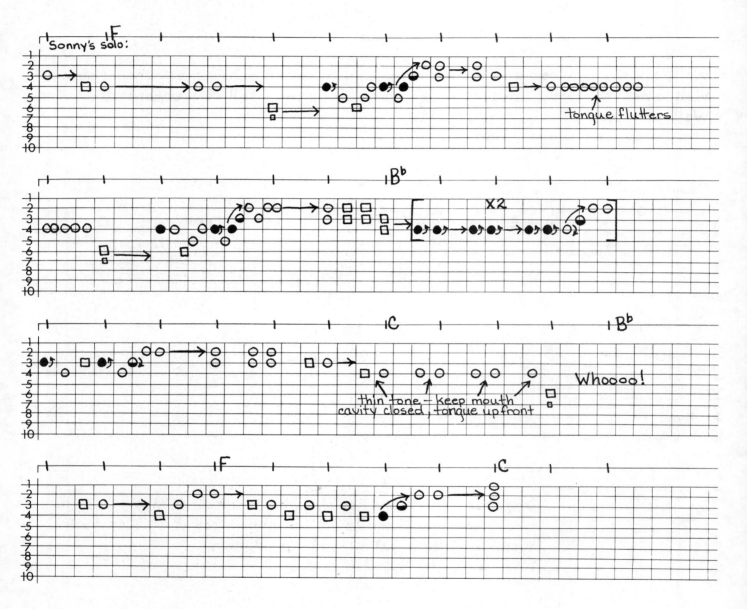

Sonny's solo:

tongue flutters

Whoooo!

thin tone – keep mouth
cavity closed, tongue up front

7th Verse :
Well, I'm gonna sing this 'a verse, and I ain't gonna sing it no more.
Well, I'm gonna sing this 'a verse, and I ain't gonna sing it no more.
Well, I heard my good girl call me,
You know I'm hooked and I'm 'bout to go.

Baby, I Knocked On Your Door

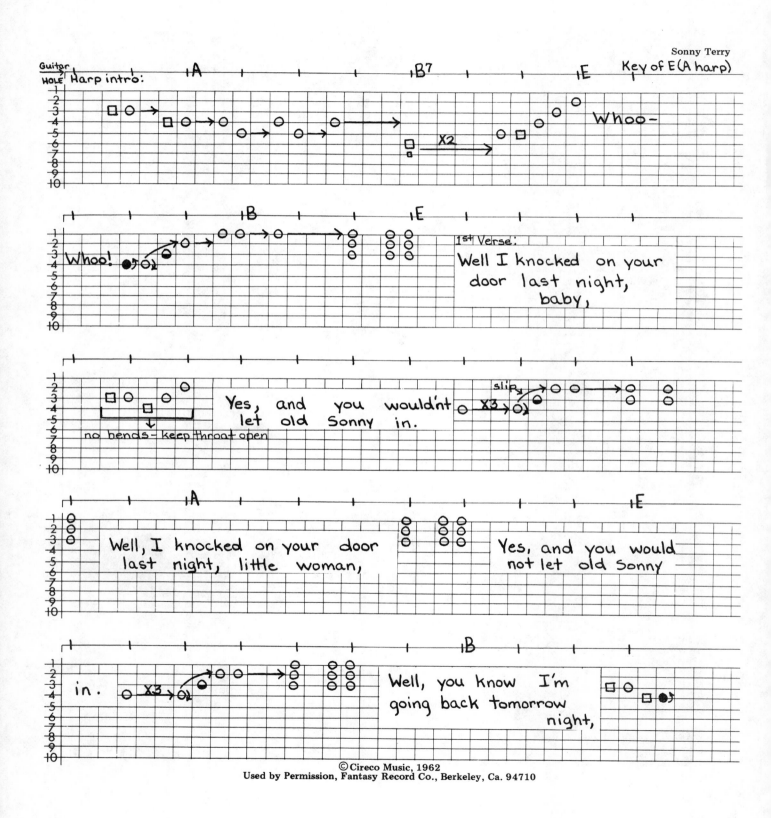

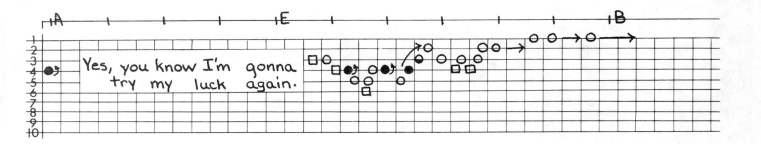

Well, I done told you, little woman,
   (harp ride)
Well, you know I ain't gonna tell
   you no more. *(harp ride)*
Well, I done told you, little woman,
   (harp ride)
Well, you know I ain't gonna tell
   you no more. *(harp ride)*
Well, you know the good book said
   you gonna, *(harp ride)*
Whoa, reap just what you sow.
   (turnaround)

You know, I give you all my money,
I can't stand the way you do.
You know, I give you all my money,
I can't stand the way you do.
Well, you know you have been a
   good little girl,
Whoa, but you just won't be true.

Well, I'm gonna buy me a pistol,
   little woman,
Made up on a forty-four frame,
Well, I'm gonna buy me a pistol,
   little woman,
Made up on a forty-four frame.
Well, you can look down in the
   ground, little woman,
Whoa, you know you can see that
   undertaker man.

Well, you know I feel like snapping,
   baby,
Yes, my pistol all in your face.
Well, you know I feel like snapping,
   baby,
Yes, my pistol all in your face.
Well, you know some old lonely
   graveyard,
Yes, will be your resting place.

My Baby Leavin'

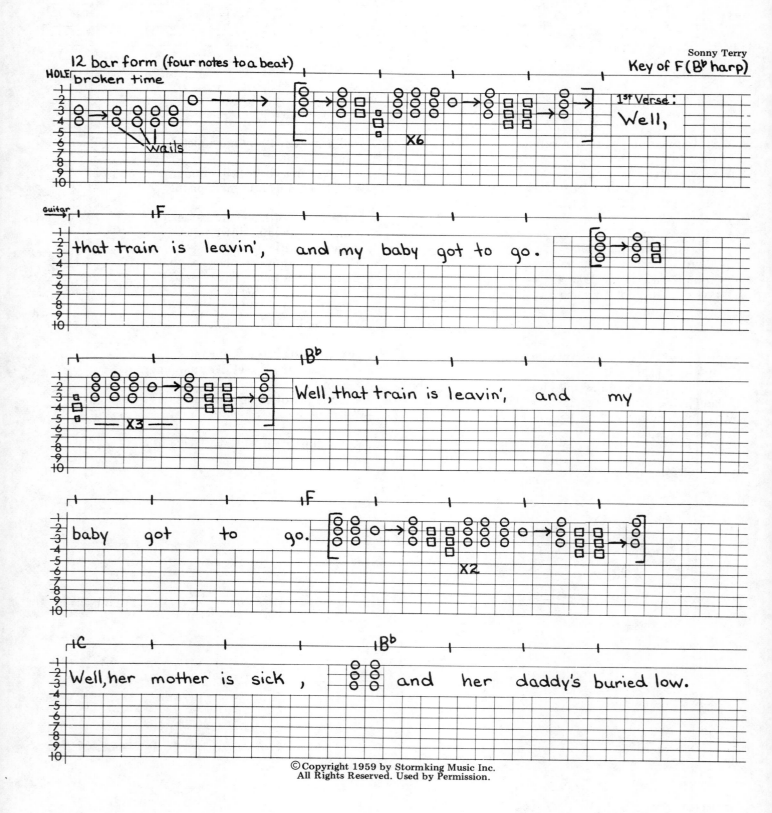

2nd Verse:
Well I watched that train, till it went around the bend. (Chugging)
Well I watched that train, till it went around the bend. (Chugging)
Well I said I. would never, see my baby's face again.

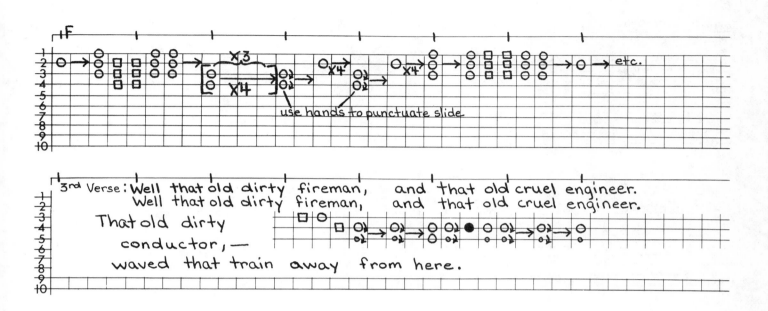

use hands to punctuate slide

3rd Verse: Well that old dirty fireman,   and that old cruel engineer.
Well that old dirty fireman,   and that old cruel engineer.
That old dirty
conductor, —
waved that train away from here.

4th Verse:
Everytime I hear that whistle, Lord I just can't keep from crying. (Harp chugging)
Everytime I hear that whistle, Lord I just can't keep from crying. (Harp chugging)
Well, that ol' dirty train, got that ol' gal I call mine.

5th Verse:
If I could holler, just 'a like a mountain jack. (Harp chugging)
If I could holler, just 'a like a mountain jack. (Harp chugging)
I'd go way up on that mountain, call my lovin' baby back.
Wanna call her back, wanna call her back, wanna call her back, wanna call her back.

Jailhouse Blues

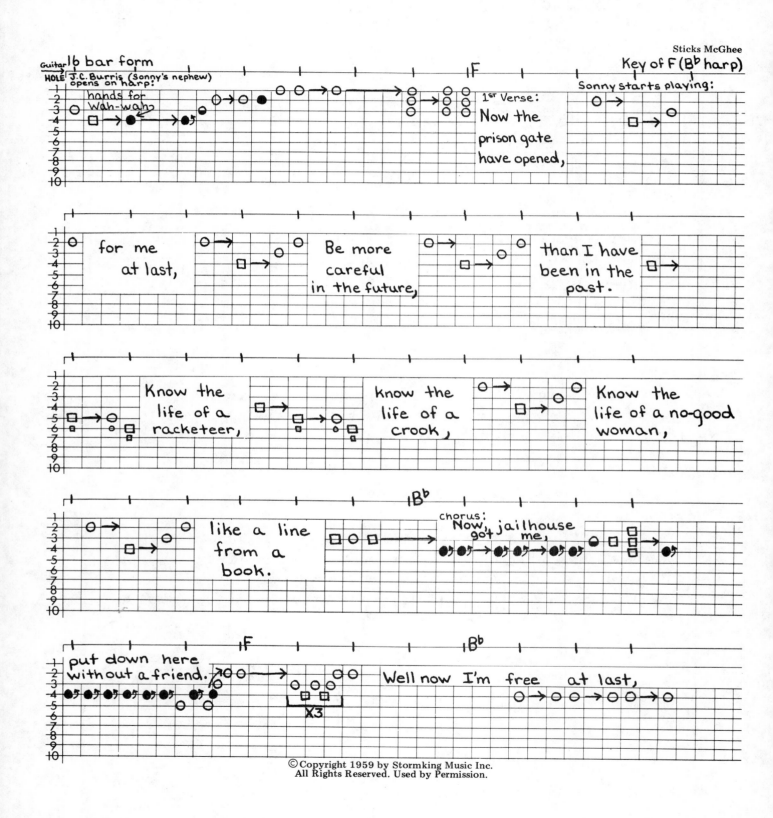

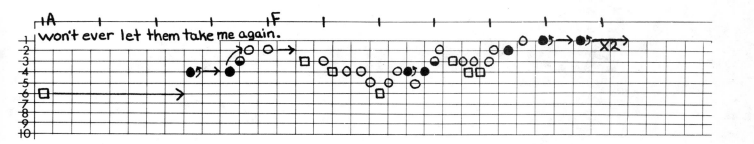
won't ever let them take me again.

Had a girl one time, wouldn't work
  or steal,
Broad came right out 'a, Mississippi
  cotton field.
She wouldn't steal, on the verge of
  a doubt,
But she get you busted, wouldn't
  get you out.

Chorus:

Come down to your jail, think you
  all rich,
Not to go to your bail, see how much
  time you gone get.
When the judge sentence you, mighty
  near a smile,
Know you'll be gone, for a long, long
  while.

Chorus:

After you up the river, 'bout a month
  or more,
You receive a letter from that gal
  you used to know.
'Bout three feet wide, nine page long,
Whole lotta talk 'bout what's goin' on.

Chorus:

The letter said, "Daddy, things out here
  have gotten mighty tight,
Had to rob two guys, before I could eat
  last night.
Meant to send you some money, but to
  my surprise,
I'd already sealed your letter, and the
  gum 'a had dried."

Chorus:

Poor Man But A Good Man

Sonny Terry and J. C. Burris
Key of E (A harp)

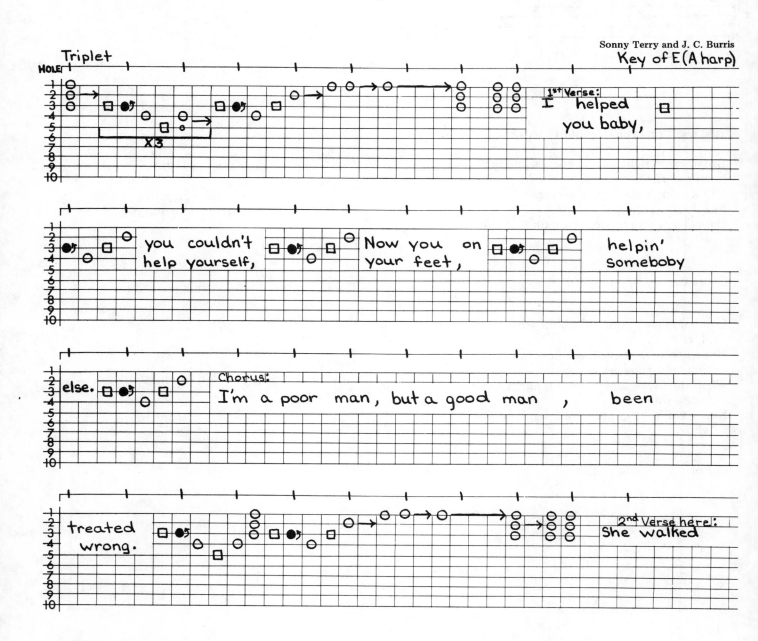

2nd Verse:
She walked off and left me, she didn't say a word,
Wasn't nothin' she knowed, but somethin' she heard.

Chorus:

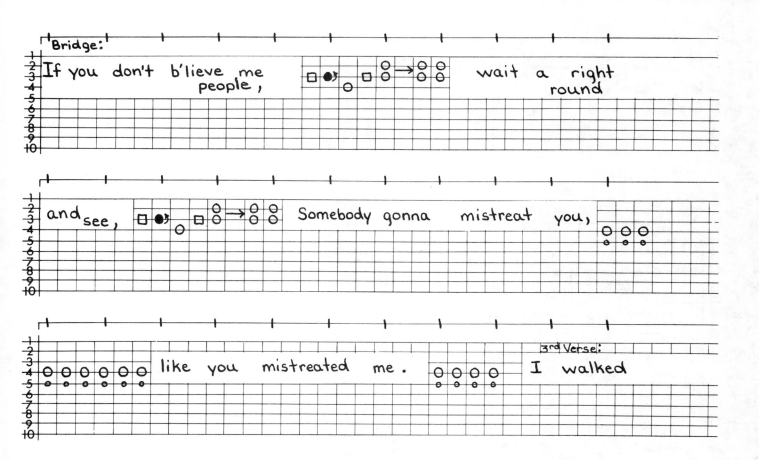

3rd Verse:

I walked down to the station, I looked up on the wall,
My money was too light, I didn't go nowhere at all.

Chorus:

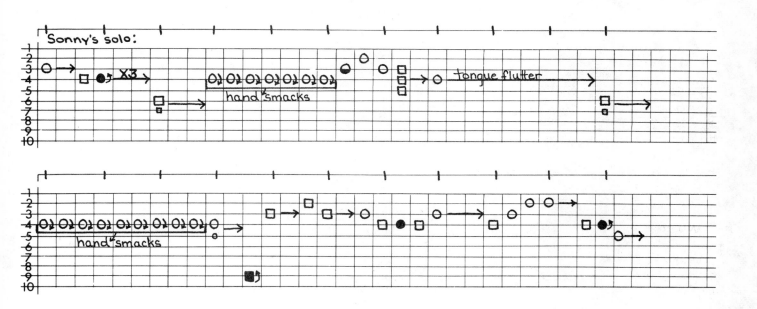

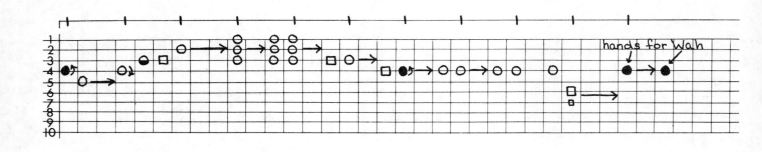

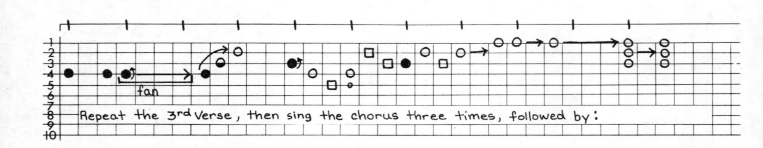

Repeat the 3rd Verse, then sing the chorus three times, followed by:

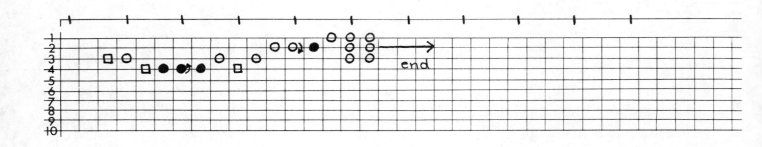

Left to right—Sonny, Memphis Slim and Brownie at the Newport Folk Festival, 1959.

All Alone Blues

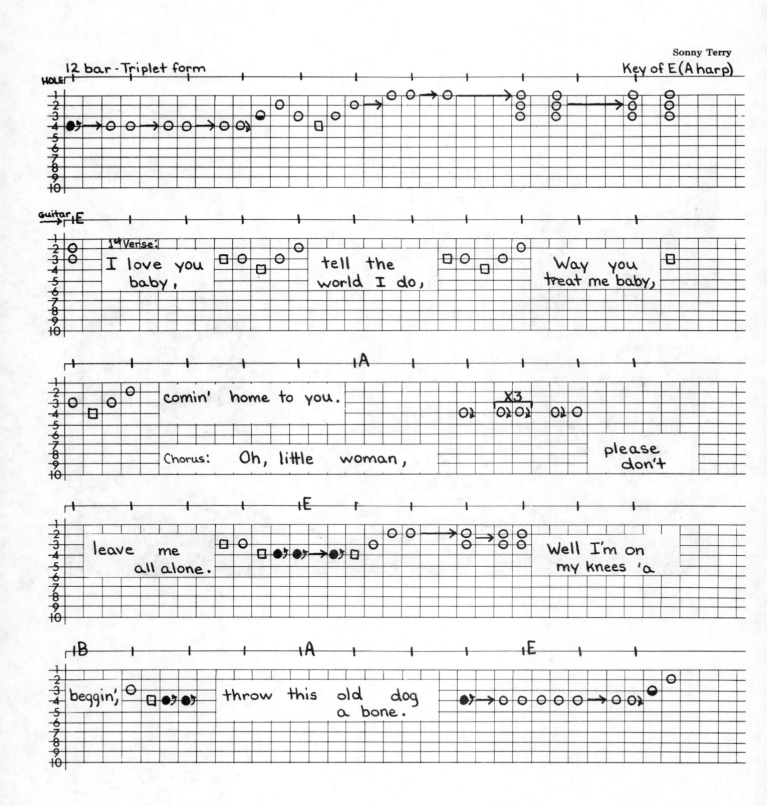

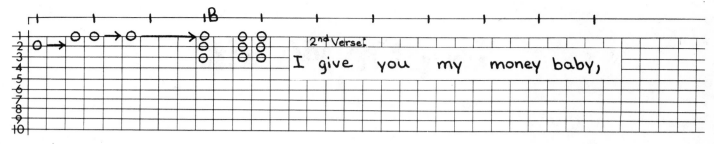

2ⁿᵈ Verse:

I give you my money baby, I need shoes on my feet,
Now you got me down, you want to throw me in the street.

Chorus:

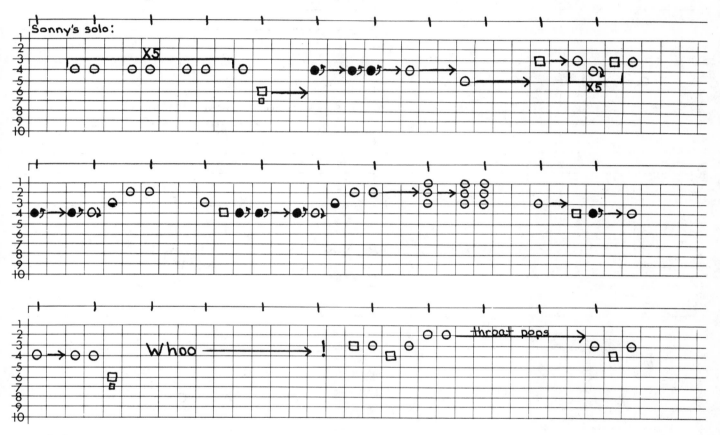

3ʳᵈ Verse:

Always told you, baby, time and time again,
Honey you know I ain't too innocent, I'd rather be your friend.

Chorus:

4ᵗʰ Verse:

I give you my money baby, with all that's true,
So you mistreat me baby, that the way you want to do.

Keep On Walkin'

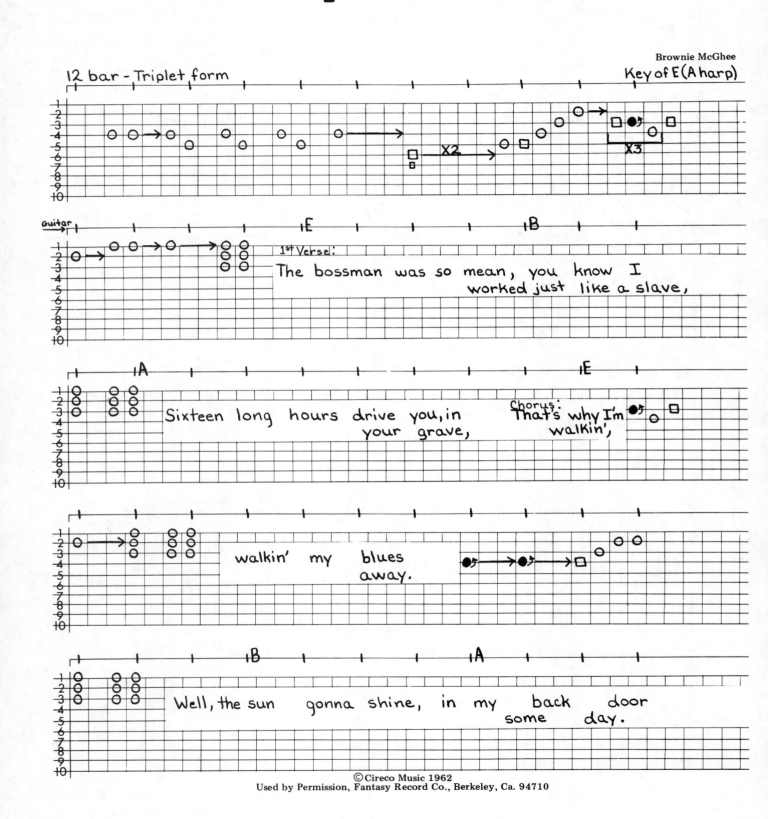

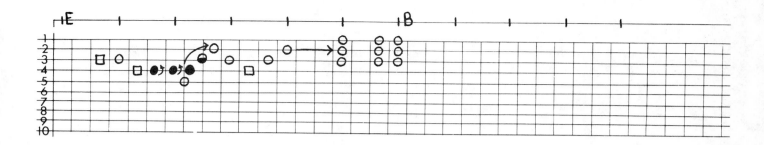

2nd Verse :
You can't plant cotton and expect to gather corn,
Can't take right peoples, and sure make it wrong,

Chorus :

3rd Verse :
I once had a car, it was painted white and black,
Couldn't keep up the payments, the man he come and took it back,

Chorus :

4th Verse :
I wouldn't tell a mule to get up, if he set down in my lap,
Yes that's what killed my old grandpap,

Chorus :

5th Verse :
I got them old coffee grounds in my coffee, big boweevals in my fields,
Tacks in my shoes keep on stickin' me, in my heels,

Chorus :

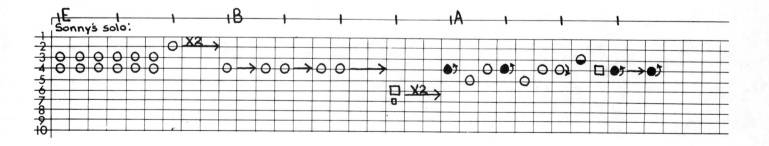

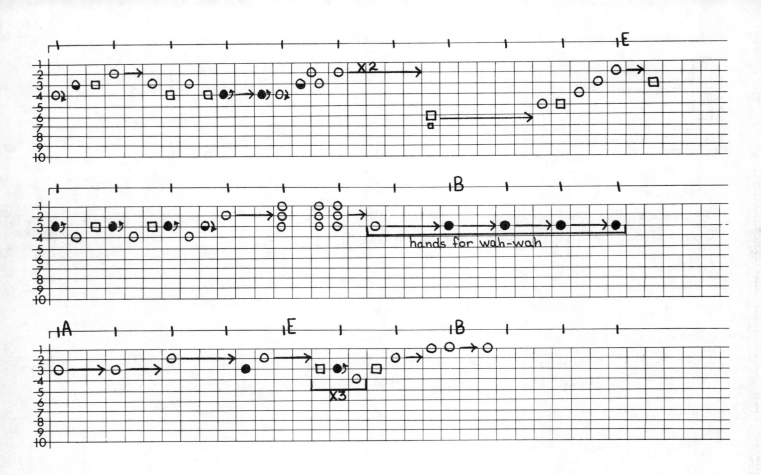

6th Verse: Brownie McGhee sings:

You used to be my sweet milk, now you sour on me,
Since we're not together, you're not sweet like you used to be,

Chorus:

7th Verse: Brownie sings:

Paper boy hollerin' extree, have you read the news,
Just shot the woman I love, got that walkin' blues,

Chorus: Repeat last line four times

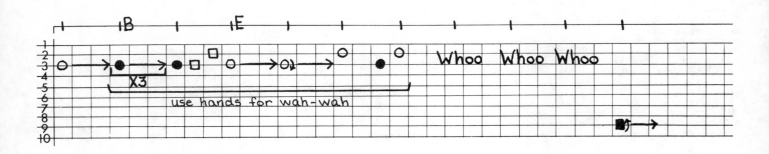

Sonny in concert with Eric Weisberg, 1960.

Telephone Blues

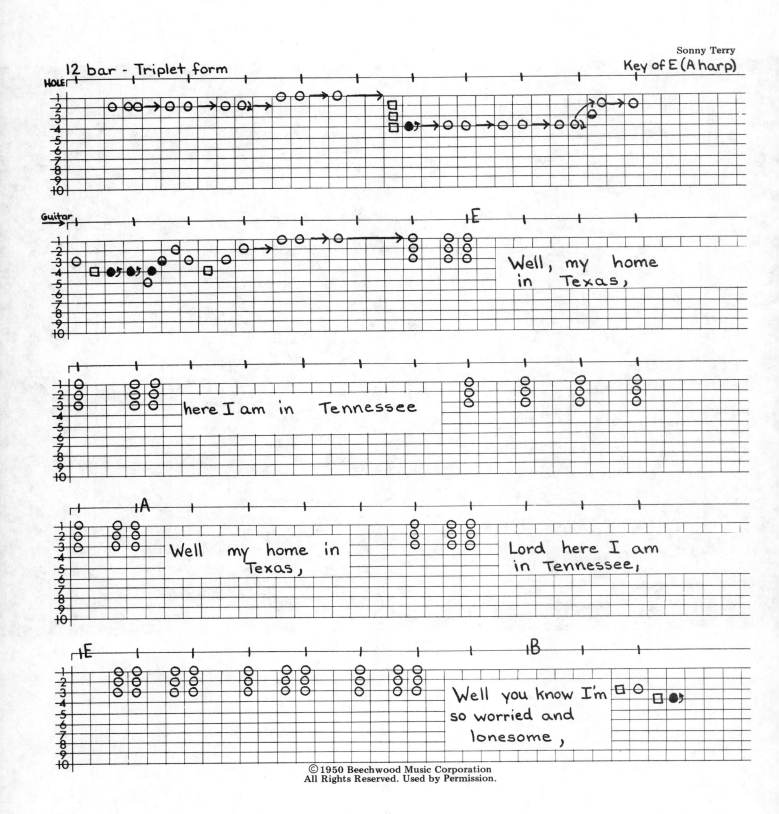

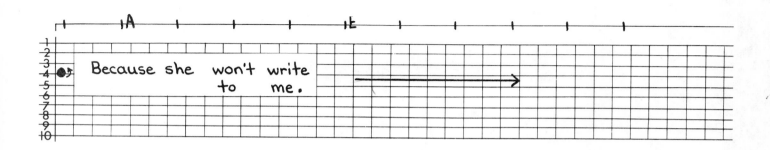

2nd Verse:
Telephone me, telephone me sweetheart, telephone me everyday,
Telephone me, telephone me sweetheart, telephone me everyday,
Well, you know I'm workin' in this town for you lil' woman,
A whoa, you know I'm sending you all my pay.
Instru. break – piano and guitar

3rd Verse:
Well, my home in Texas, Tennessee's no place for me,
Well, my home in Texas, Tennessee's no place for me,
Well, you know I'll soon be with you darlin',
A whoa please honey wait and see.

4th Verse:
My telephone won't ring, the mailman won't leave me no mail,
My telephone won't ring, the mailman won't leave me no mail,
Well, I say if I catch you cheatin' on me darlin'
A whoa, you know I'm goin' to the county jail.

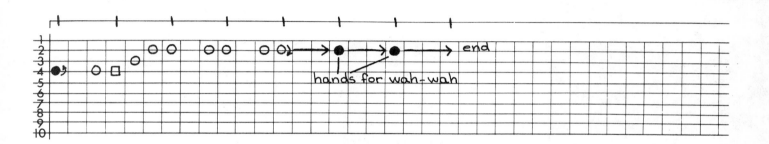

Don't Mistreat Me

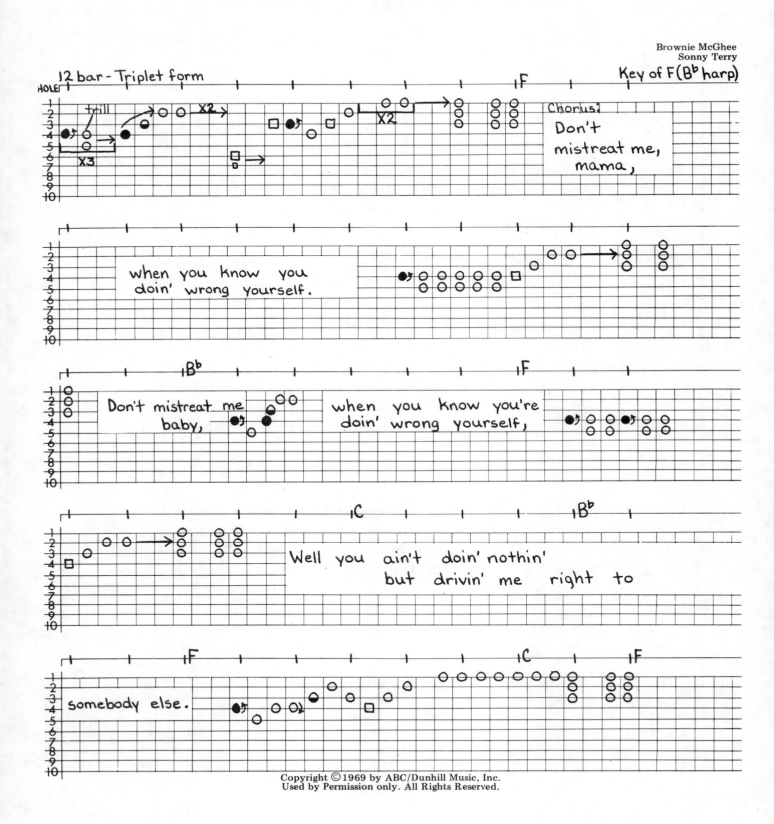

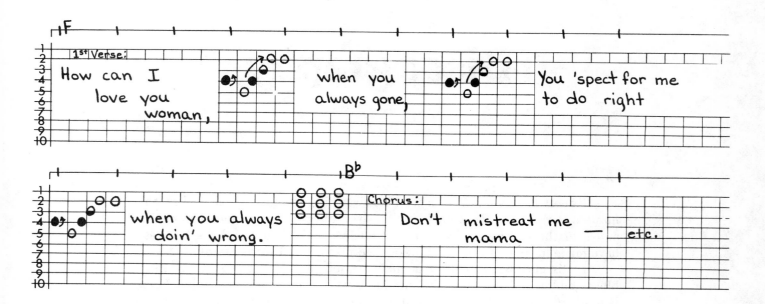

2nd Verse:
I asked her where she been, she said, "Sonny that ain't a rule".
She looked me dead in my face, "None of your business, fool".

Chorus:

3rd Verse:
You know I love you woman, you can bet your life it's true,
I want you to love me little girl, that all I want from you.

Chorus:

4th Verse:
Don't get mad little girl, cause a' the things I'm saying to you,
I want you to realize woman, you know you got some troubles, too.

Chorus:

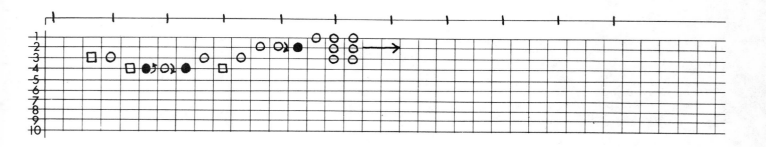

Discography

by Robert Javors

Robert Javors' interest in the blues was kindled in his teens. He has lent numerous rare records from his extensive collection to various companies active in the reissue market. Frequent trips to the South and the Midwest have made his one of the best blues collections in the United States.

He is currently involved in many varied projects among which are a blues bibliography (with the noted West German blues scholar Leibl Rosenberg), a Chicago blues guitar primer (with Oak Publications editor Arthur Steinman), and a guide for blues collectors.

Explanatory Notes

The discography that follows lists all the recordings in which Sonny Terry appeared, either as the featured artist or as an accompanyist. All sessions are listed chronologically under the name of the artist to whom the original recording was credited. An italicized label name indicates an extended or long playing recording. All others are either 45 or 78 r.p.m. recordings. A letter in parentheses after the label name indicates the label's country of origin. Lack of a letter indicates a U.S. pressing. Due to the tremendous increase in blues reissues worldwide, it is impossible to list every reissue, nor is it very desirable. Most foreign issues and reissues listed here can be obtained both here and abroad without too much effort.

Abbreviations

Countries of Origin

A   — Austria
D   — Denmark
E   — England
Fr   — France
G   — Germany
Sw — Sweden

Record Labels

ARC — American Record Company
            (Includes labels such as
            Oriole, Banner, Romeo,
            Perfect, Melotone, etc.)
Co   — Columbia
Cq   — Conqueror
LC   — Library of Congress
Vo   — Vocalion

Instruments

bjo   — banjo
bs   — bass
cl   — clarinet
dms — drums
gtr   — guitar
hca   — harmonica
org   — organ
pno   — piano
tbn   — trombone
ten   — tenor sax
tpt   — trumpet
vcl   — vocal
vln   — violin
wbd — washboard

Acknowledgements

    The two books constantly referred to for the proper completion of this discography were: *Blues Records: 1943-66* by the late blues scholar Mike Leadbitter and Neil Slaven published by Hanover Books Ltd. in England in 1968 and *Blues & Gospel Records 1902-42* in England in 1964 and later revised in 1969. Without these two pioneering works blues scholarship would still be in its infancy.

NOTE: *Blues Records* is available through Oak Publications, 33 West 60th Street, or from your local bookstore.

BLIND BOY FULLER   New York, 15 December 1937

Blind Boy Fuller, vcl/gtr; Sonny Terry, hca.

Mistreater, You're Going To Be Sorry	ARC 8-03-60, Vo 03490, Cq 9000
Bye Bye Baby Blues	Vo 04843; *RBF* 9, *Blues Classics* 11
Looking For My Woman No. 2	Vo 04054, Cq 9038

New York, 16 December 1937

I'm Going To Move (To The Edge Of Town)	ARC 8-02-66, Vo 03457, Cq 9012

New York, 5 April 1938

Pistol Slapper Blues	Vo 04106, Cq 9075, Co 30083, 37781; *Blues Classics* 11
Mean And No Good Woman	Vo 04106, Cq 9075, Co 30083, 37781; *Matchbox* (E) 143
Georgia Ham Mama	Vo 04315
Mama Let Me Lay It On You No. 2	Vo 04237, Cq 9158

Poss. Columbia, S.C., 29 Oct. 1938

Blind Boy Fuller, vcl/gtr; Sonny Terry, hca; prob. own kazoo-1; Bull City Red, wbd-2; Bull City Red replaces Fuller on vcl-3.

You're Laughing Now	Vo 04557, Cq 9171
Stop Jivin' Me Mama	Vo 04897
Long Time Trucker	Vo 04675
Big House Bound	Vo 04897; *Blues Classics* 11
Flyin' Airplane Blues-1, 2, 3	Vo 04557, Cq 9171
Get Your Yas Yas Out-2	Vo 04519, Cq 9157, Co 30086, 37784; *Matchbox* (E) 143

SONNY TERRY   New York, December 1938

Sonny Terry, hca; some with vocal

Fox Chase	LC AAFS 19-B; *L4*
New Careless Love	LC
The New Red River Blues	LC
Louise	LC
The Freight Train	LC
Meet Me On The Railroad And Bring My Shoes and Clothes	LC
Lost John	LC AAFS 19-A, *L4*
Lost John (Alt. take)	LC AAFS 19-A, *L4*

NOTE: AAFS 19 and L4 credited to SANDERS TERRY.

New York, 24 December 1938

Sonny Terry, vcl/hca; Oh Red, wbd-1

Mountain Blues	*Vanguard* (E) 8524, *Top Rank* (E) 35065, *Fontana* (E & D) 5188, *AURS* (G) 9015, *Vanguard* 25/26,
The New John Henry-1	*Vanguard* (E) 8524, *Top Rank* (E) 35065, *Fontana* (E & D) 5188, *AURS* (G) 9015

BLIND BOY FULLER   Memphis, 12 July 1939

Blind Boy Fuller, vcl/gtr; Sonny Terry, hca; Oh Red, wbd-1

I Don't Care How Long	Vo 05273
I'm A Stranger Here	Vo 05273
I Want Some Of Your Pie-1	Vo 05030, Cq 9310, Co 30060, 37683; *Columbia* 30008
Jivin' Big Bill Blues	Vo 05218
Woman You Better Wake Up	Vo 05150, Cq 9344

BROTHER GEORGE   Memphis, 12 July 1939
(Blind Boy Fuller) AND HIS
SANCTIFIED SINGERS

Vcl trio with Sonny Terry and Oh Red, acc. by Blind Boy Fuller, gtr; Oh Red, wbd-1.

Have You Decided (Which Way To Go)-1	OK 05893
I See The Sign Of Judgement-1	Vo 05261; *Blues Classics* 18
Everybody Wants To Know How I Die-1	OK 06019, Cq 9361

SONNY JONES   Memphis, 12 July 1939

Sonny Jones, vcl/gtr; Sonny Terry, hca; Oh Red, wbd.

I'm Pretty Good At It	Vo 05124

BROTHER GEORGE   Memphis, 13 July 1939
(Blind Boy Fuller) AND HIS
SANCTIFIED SINGERS

Vcl trio with Sonny Terry and Oh Red, acc. by Blind Boy Fuller, gtr; Oh Red, wbd-1.

I Feel Like Shoutin'	Vo 05261, Cq 9361
Jesus Touched Me-1	OK 06019
Talkin' With Jesus-1	OK 05893

BLIND BOY FULLER   New York, 5 March 1940

Blind Boy Fuller, vcl/gtr; Sonny Terry, hca; Oh Red, wbd-1.

Blue And Worried Man-1	Vo 05440, Cq 9373

SONNY TERRY   New York, 5 March 1940

Sonny Terry, hca; acc. by Oh Red, wbd-1.

Harmonica Blues	OK 05453, Cq 9382, Co 30063, 37686; *Flyright* (E) 107
Harmonica And Washboard Breakdown-1	OK 05453, Cq 9382, Co 30063, 37686; *Roots* (A) 321, *Folkways* 2801, 2804

BLIND BOY FULLER   New York, 6 March 1940

Blind Boy Fuller, vcl/gtr; Sonny Terry, hca; Oh Red, wbd-1.

Somebody's Been Talkin'-1	Vo 05527, Cq 9376; *Roots* (A) 318
Three Ball Blues	Vo 05440, Cq 9373; *Blues Classics* 11

SONNY TERRY   New York, 6 March 1940

Sonny Terry, hca; acc. by Oh Red, wbd-1; allegedly Blind Boy Fuller, gtr-2.

Harmonica Stomp-1, 2	OK 05538, Co 30064, 37687; *Xtra* (E) 1035, *Folkways* 202
Harmonica And Washboard Blues-1	OK 05538, Co 30064, 37687; *Flyright* (E) 106

BLIND BOY FULLER   New York, 7 March 1940

Blind Boy Fuller, vcl/gtr; Sonny Terry, hca; Sonny Terry, vcl-1; Oh Red, wbd-2, vcl-3.

Good Feeling Blues-2	OK 06231; *Blues Classics* 11
*You Can't Hide From The Lord-1, 2, 3	Vo 05465
*Twelve Gates To The City-2	Vo 05465

NOTE: Sides marked * are labelled BROTHER GEORGE AND HIS SANCTIFIED SINGERS

Chicago, 19 June 1940

Blind Boy Fuller, vcl/gtr; Sonny Terry, hca; Oh Red, wbd-1.

I Don't Want No Skinny Woman-1	OK 05657, Cq 9377, Co 30090, 37788; *Flyright* (E) 105
Bus Rider Blues-1	OK 05933, Cq 9757; *Blues Classics* 11
You Got To Have Your Dollar	OK 05712, Cq 9758; *Historical* 31
Bye Bye Baby	OK 05712, Cq 9758
*Precious Lord-1	OK 05729

NOTE: side marked * is labelled BROTHER GEORGE AND HIS SANCTIFIED SINGERS

SONNY TERRY   Chicago, 19 June 1940

Sonny Terry, hca; acc. by Oh Red, wbd-1; Blind Boy Fuller, vcl-2.

Forty-Four Whistle Blues-2	OK 05684
Blowing The Blues-1	OK 05684

BROWNIE MCGHEE   New York, 22 October 1941

Brownie McGhee, vcl/gtr; Sonny Terry, hca; Jordan Webb, hca-1; Robert Young, wbd-2.

Goodbye Now-1, 2	Co unissued
Working Man's Blues-2	OK 06698, Co 30027, 37460

BUDDY MOSS   **New York, 22 October 1941**

Buddy Moss, acc. by self or Brownie McGhee, gtr; Sonny Terry,
hca; Oh Red, wbd.

You Started It, Woman	Co unissued
Give Me My Loving	Co unissued
Wrong Kind Of Women Blues	Co unissued

SONNY TERRY AND   **New York, 22 October 1941**
JORDAN WEBB

Presumably vcl, acc. Sonny Terry, hca; Jordan Webb, hca (prob
alternate vcls with hca acc).

My Baby's So Sweet	OK unissued
Touch It Up And Go	OK unissued
Weary Worried Blues	OK unissued
What Do You Know Joe	OK unissued

BROWNIE McGHEE   **New York, 23 October 1941**

Brownie McGhee, vcl/gtr; Sonny Terry, hca; Jordan Webb, hca-1

Back Home Blues-1	OK 06579, Co 30031, 37464
It Must Be Love	OK 06579, Co 30031, 37464

HUDDIE LEADBELLY   **Washington, D.C., May 1942**

Huddie Ledbetter (Leadbelly), vcl/gtr; Brownie McGhee, gtr;
Sonny Terry, hca.

T. B. Blues	LC

BROWNIE McGHEE   **Washington, D.C., May 1942**

Brownie McGhee, vcl/gtr; Sonny Terry, hca; Leadbelly, gtr; or
vcl duet by McGhee and Terry. Acc. uncertain-1.

Railroad Bill-1	LC
Interview	LC
How Long	LC

SONNY TERRY   **Washington, D.C., May 1942**

Sonny Terry, vcl, presumably acc. own hca; Brownie McGhee and
Huddie Ledbetter added-1.

Worry Blues	LC
The Brain	LC
So Sweet	LC
John Henry-1	LC, *Folkways* 2801
Fox Chase	LC
The Red Cross	LC

CHAMPION JACK DUPREE   **New York City, 1942**

Champion Jack Dupree, vcl/pno; Sonny Terry, hca; Brownie
McGhee, gtr.

Slow Boogie	*Folkways* FJ 2801, FP 53
Jitterbug	*Folkways* FJ 2804, FP 59
Mexican Reminiscences	*Folkways* FP 71

New York City, Summer 1943

Champion Jack Dupree, vcl/pno; Sonny Terry, hca.

Black Woman Blues	Solo 10-014

LEADBELLY   **New York City, Summer 1943**

Leadbelly, vcl/gtr; Sonny Terry, hca.

On A Monday	Asch 343-3; *Stinson* 17; *Melodisc* (E) 1187, EPM 7-77; *Storyville* (E) 616.003; *Design* 903, 247; *Storyville* (D) 124;
John Henry	Asch 343-3; same as above
How Long Blues	Asch 343-1; *Stinson* 17; *Melodisc* (E) 1140, EPM 7-63; *Storyville* (D) 124, SEP 337; *Storyville* (E) 616.003; *Design* 903, 247
Irene (Goodnight Irene)	Asch 343-2, Atlantic 917; *Stinson* 17; *Atlantic* SD 8161
Irene (Alternate take)	*Melodisc* (E) 1151, EPM 7-63; *Storyville* (D) SEP 337, 139
Ain't You Glad	Asch 343-2; *Stinson* 17; *Design* 903, 247; *Melodisc* (E) 1151; EPM 7-63; *Storyville* (D) SEP 337, 139

Good Morning Blues	Asch 343-1, Atlantic 917; *Stinson* 17; *Melodisc* (E) 1140, EPM 7-63; *Storyville* (D) SEP 337, 124; *Storyville* (E) 616.003

SONNY TERRY   **New York City, 1944**

Sonny Terry, vcl/hca; Woody Guthrie, gtr.

Glory	Asch 432-2
Lonesome Train	Asch 550-3; *Asch* LP AA1

LEADBELLY   **New York City, mid 1944**

Leadbelly, vcl/gtr; Sonny Terry, hca.

In The Evenin' When The Sun Goes Down	*Stinson* 48; *Musidisc* (E) 12-107; *Storyville* (D) 124; *Storyville* (E) 616.003

BROWNIE McGHEE &   **New York City, 12 December 1944**
SONNY TERRY

Brownie McGhee, vcl/gtr; Sonny Terry, hca.

That's The Stuff (Watch Out)	Savoy 5533, 826
Knockabout Blues (Carolina Blues)	Savoy 5533, 826
Easy Ridin' Buggy	Savoy 5534
Woman Lover Blues	Savoy 5534

SUNNY TERRY

Sonny Terry, vcl/hca; Brownie McGhee, gtr.

Run Away Women (Hootin' The Blues	Savoy 5549, 850
Shake Down (Shake Down Blues)	Savoy 5549, 850

SONNY TERRY   **New York City, 1945**

Sonny Terry, vcl/hca; Brownie McGhee, gtr.

Sweet Woman	Solo 10-004
Fox Chase (no gtr)	Solo 10-004

BROWNIE McGHEE   **New York City, 1946**

Brownie McGhee, vcl/gtr; Sonny Terry, hca; Melvin Merritt, pno;
Pops Foster or Count Edmondson, bs; Sticks Evans, dms; Jesse
Powell, ten-1.

Going Down Slow	Alert 405
Brownie's Guitar Boogie	Alert 403, 405
Rock Me Mama	Alert 402
Night Time Is The Right Time	Alert 404; *Bluesland* (E) 2
Worried Life Blues	Alert 403
Lovin' With A Feeling	Alert 404; *Bluesland* (E) 2
No Worries On My Brain	Alert 402
Key To The Highway	Alert 400; *Bluesland* (E) 2
Mean Ole Frisco	Alert 401
Rum Cola Papa	Alert 400
Sportin' Life Blues	Alert 401; *Xtra* (E) 1035; *Folkways* 202
Bad Blood	Alert 406
I Don't Care	Alert 406
Strange Woman	Alert 407
Big Legged Woman	Alert 407
Greyhound Bus	Alert 408
Confusin' Blues	Alert 408
B. M. Blues	Alert 409
Evil But Kindhearted	Alert 409
Shake It Up And Go	Alert 410
Brownie Blues	Alert 410
Good Stem Winder	Alert 411
My Mary Blues	Alert 411
Best Jelly Roll In Town	Alert 412
Seaboard And Southern	Alert 412; *Flyright* (E) 4705
Dissatisfied Woman	Alert 413
Hello Blues	Alert 420
How Can I Love You	Alert 420
Baseball Boogie-1	Alert 413
One For The Money	Alert 413

NOTE: Alert 413 was issued with both One For The Money and
Dissatisfied Woman backing Baseball Boogie.

SONNY TERRY   **New York City, January, 1947**

Sonny Terry, vcl/hca; Brownie McGhee, gtr; Baby Dodds, dms.

Whoopin' The Blues	Capitol 40003; *Capitol* T793, 20906; *Pickwick* 3173
Leavin' Blues	Capitol 40043; *Capitol* 20906; *Pickwick* 3173
Riff And Harmonica Jump	Capitol 40061; *Capitol* 20906
All Alone Blues	Capitol 40003; *Capitol* 20906; *Pickwick* 3173

New York City, 30 March 1947

Sonny Terry, hca; Alan Gilbert and Lynn Murray's Singers, vcl; Orch acc.

This Time Of The Year	*Columbia* 4392M

New York City, 12 June 1947

Sonny Terry, vcl/hca; Brownie McGhee, gtr; Baby Dodds, dms.

Harmonica Rag	Capitol 15237; *Capitol* 20906
Screamin' And Cryin' Blues	Capitol 40061; *Capitol* 20906
Beer Garden Blues	Capitol 40097; *Capitol* 20906
Worried Man Blues	Capitol 40043; *Capitol* 20906

New York City, 13 November 1947

Sonny Terry, vcl/hca; Melvin Merritt, pno; Brownie McGhee, gtr; bs; dms.

Hot Headed Woman	Capitol 40122; *Capitol* 20906
Custard Pie Blues	Capitol 40122; *Capitol* 20906
Crow Jane Blues	Capitol 40097; *Capitol* 20906
Early Morning Blues	Capitol 15237; *Capitol* 20906

BROWNIE McGHEE   **New York City, 1948**

Brownie McGhee, vcl/gtr; Sonny Terry, hca; Tiny Parker, pno; Bob Harris, bs; dms.

Sweet Baby Blues	Savoy 899; *Savoy 12218*
4 O'Clock In The Morning	Savoy 899; *Savoy* 12218

SONNY TERRY   **New York City, early 1950**

Sonny Terry, vcl/hca; Wilbert Ellis, pno; Brownie McGhee, gtr; Melvin Merritt, dms.

Telephone Blues	Capitol 931; *Capitol* 20906; *Pickwick* 3173
Tell Me, Tell Me	unissued
Dirty Mistreater	Capitol 931; *Capitol* 20906; *Pickwick* 3173

STICKS McGHEE   **New York City, March, 1950**

Sticks McGhee, vcl/gtr; Sonny Terry, hca; Harry "Van" Walls, pno; bs; dms.

Let's Do It	Atlantic 912
She's Gone	Atlantic 912
House Warmin' Boogie	Atlantic 926
Blue Barrelhouse	Atlantic 937

SONNY TERRY   **New York City, 1951/2**

Sonny Terry, vcl/hca; Doc Bagby, org; Brownie McGhee, gtr; Melvin Merritt, dms.

Baby Let's Have Some Fun	Gotham 517
Four O'Clock Blues	Gotham 517
Harmonica Rhumba	Gotham 518
Lonesome Room	Gotham 518
No Love Blues	Unissued
Wine Headed Woman	Unissued

SONNY TERRY TRIO

Sonny Terry, vcl/hca; Brownie McGhee, gtr; Coyal McMahan, bongos.

Hootin Blues	Gramercy 1004
Dangerous Woman	Gramercy 1005

SONNY TERRY   **New York City, 1952**

Sonny Terry, vcl/hca.

Dirty Mistreater	*Aravel* 1004; *Ember* (E) 4562
Alcoholic Blues	*Folkways* Fp 35, 2035; *Topic* (E) 10T30
Women's Blues (Corrina)	—
Lost John	—
Locomotive Blues	—
Bad Luck Blues	—
Harmonica Stomp	—
Shortnin' Bread	—
Fine And False Voice	—
Beautiful City	*Ember* (E) 4562

Sonny Terry, vcl-2/hca; Woody Guthrie, vcl-1/gtr; Brownie McGhee, gtr-4; no vocals-3.

Silver Fox Chase-1	*Stinson* 55, *Melodisc* 516, 7-83
Don't You Hear Me Calling You Blues-2	*Stinson* 55
Worried And Lonesome Blues-2	—
She Is A Sweet Woman-2	—
South Bend Express-3	— *Melodisc* 7-83
You Don't Want Me Blues-2	*Stinson* 55
Tell Me Little Woman-3	—
Greyhound Bus Blues-4	—

Sonny Terry, vcl/hca; Brownie McGhee, Leadbelly, Cisco Houston, Pete Seeger, or Woody Guthrie, gtrs.

A Man Is Nothing But A Fool	Verve 9010
Right On That Shore	—
Louise	—
John Henry	—
Go Tell Aunt Rhody	—
Good Morning Blues	—
Twelve Gates To The City	—
Easy Rider	—
Careless Love	—
Key To The Highway	—

Sonny Terry, vcl-1/hca; Alex Seward, vcl-2/gtr; Wood Guthrie, vcl-3/gtr; Vcl chorus-4; no hca-5; no gtrs-6.

Cornbread, Meat & Molasses-4, 5	*Archive of Folk Music* 106, 206; *Ember* (E) 136	
Ham & Eggs-4	—	
Lost John-1, 3	—	—
Chain Gang Blues-1, 3	—	—
It Takes A Chain Gang Man-4	—	—
Betty & Dupree-2	—	—
Stockhole-3	—	—
Rock Me Mama-2	—	—
Chain Gang Special-3	—	—
Long John-3, 5, 6	—	—
Pick A Bale Of Cotton-1, 3	—	—
Red River-1, 3	—	—

Sonny Terry, vcl/hca; wbd; washtub; bones; frying pans.

The Woman Is Killing Me	Folkways FP6, FA 2006	
Custard Pie	—	
Diggin' My Patatoes	—	—
Man Is A Crazy Fool	—	—
Wine Headed Woman	—	—
My Baby Is Goin' to Change The Lock	—	—
Sonny's Jump	—	—
Louise Blues	—	—

SONNY "HOOTIN" TERRY

Sonny Terry, vcl/hca; Brownie McGhee, gtr.

I Don't Worry	Jax 305
Man Ain't Nothing But A Fool	—

SONNY TERRY & HIS BUCKSHOT FIVE

Sonny Terry, vcl/hca; Bob Gaddy, pno; Brownie McGhee, gtr; Bob Harris, bs; Gene Brooks, dms.

Dangerous Woman (With A 45 In Her Hand)	Harlem 2327
I Love You Baby	

SONNY "HOOTIN' " TERRY & HIS NIGHT OWLS

Sonny Terry, vcl/hca; Brownie McGhee, gtr; Bob Gaddy or Wilbert Ellis, pno; dms.

That Woman Is Killing Me	Jackson 2302; *Bluesland* (E) 2
Harmonica Train	Jackson 2302; *Bluesland* (E) 2
	Blues Classics 23

ALLEN BUNN   New York City, 1952

Allen Bunn, vcl/gtr; Sonny Terry, hca; Wilbert Ellis, pno.

She'll Be Sorry	Apollo 436
The Guy With The "45"	Apollo 436; *Flyright* (E) 4705
Discouraged	Apollo 439; *Blues Obscurities* (E) 6

BOB GADDY & HIS ALLEY CATS   New York City, c. 1952

Bob Gaddy, vcl/pno; Sonny Terry, hca; Brownie McGhee, gtr; dms; female vcl-1.

I (Believe You Got A Sidekick)-1	Jackson 2303
Bicycle Boogie	Jackson 2303; *Flyright* (E) 4703

BROWNIE McGHEE and his SUGAR MEN   New York City, c. 1952

Brownie McGhee, vcl/gtr; Sonny Terry, hca.

Mean Old Frisco	Jackson 2304

BROWNIE McGHEE and his JOOK BLOCK BUSTERS   New York City, 1952

Brownie McGhee, vcl/gtr; Sonny Terry, vcl-1/hca; Bob Gaddy, pno; Bob Harris, bs; George Woods, dms. Vcl by band-2.

A Letter To Lightnin' Hopkins (Lightnin's Blues)	SIW 302; *Mainstream* S6049, 308
Smiling And Crying Blues (Crying The Blues)	SIW 302; *Mainstream* S6049, 308
Meet You In The Morning-2	Jax 307; *Mainstream* S6049, 308
I Feel So Good (Feel So Good)	Jax 304; *Mainstream S6049,* 308
Key To The Highway	Jax 304
Brownie's Blues	Jax 307
Forgive Me	*Mainstream* S6049, 308
The Woman Is Killing Me-1	*Mainstream* S6049, 308

NOTE: SIW 3IW 302 also on Jax 302 and credited to Brownie McGhee & the Block Busters.

New York City, 1952

Brownie McGhee, vcl-1/gtr; Sonny Terry, vcl-2/hca.

Stranger's Blues (Stranger Blues)	Jax 310; *Mainstream* S6049, 308
Man Ain't Nothin' But A Fool	*Mainstream* S6049, 308
New Bad Blood (Bad Blood)	Jax 322; *Mainstream* S6049, 308
Mean Old Frisco	*Mainstream* S6049, 308
Mean Old Frisco (Alt take)	*Time* 7006, 2
Sittin' On Top Of The World	*Mainstream* S6049, 308
Goin' Down Slow	*Mainstream* S6049; *Time* 2, 7006

Brownie McGhee, vcl/gtr; Sonny Terry, hca; Bob Gaddy, pno; Bob Harris, bs; George Wood, dms; 2 saxes-1; unk tenor sax-2.

Dissatisfied Woman	Jax 310; *Time* 4
Pawnshop Blues	Jax 322; —
I'm 10,000 Years Old-2	Jax 312;
Cherry Red-2	—

BROWNIE McGHEE AND HIS JOOK HOUSE ROCKERS

Christina-1	Harlem 2323
Worrying Over You-1	—
Bluebird-1 (vcl by all)	Harlem 2329
My Confession (I Want To Thank You)	—

NOTE: Worrying Over You is credited to Brownie McGhee and His House Rockers.

RALPH WILLIS COUNTRY BOYS   New York City, February, 1952

Ralph Willis, vcl/gtr; Sonny Terry, hca; Brownie McGhee, gtr.

Cold Chills	Prestige 923

BROWNIE McGHEE   New York City, 1953

Brownie McGhee, vcl/gtr; Sonny Terry, hca; Jack Dupree, pno; Bob Harris, bs; Daddy Merritt, dms.

Don't Dog Your Woman	Red Robin 111
Daisy	—

CHAMPION JACK DUPREE   New York City, early 1953

Champion Jack Dupree, vcl/pno; Sonny Terry, hca; Sticks McGhee, gtr; Bob Harris, bs; Willie Jones, dms.

Highway Blues	Red Robin 112, Everlast 5032; *XX* (E) 716
Number Nine Blues	Red Robin 109

SONNY TERRY   New York City, 1953

Sonny Terry, vcl/hca; Alex Seward, vcl-1/gtr.

Red River	*Elektra* 14, *Washington* 702, *Riverside* 12-644, *Jazz Society* 50033, *Vogue* (E) 137
John Henry	*Elektra* 14, *Washington* 702, *Riverside* 12-644, *Jazz Society* 50033, *Vogue* (E) 137, 2326, 10
The Fox Chase	Same as above
Talking About The Blues	*Elektra* 14, *Washington* 702 *Riverside* 12-644, *Jazz Society* 50033, *Vogue* (E) 137, 10
Goodbye Leadbelly	Same as above
Moaning And Mourning Blues	*Elektra* 14, *Washington* 702, *Riverside* 12-644, *Jazz Society* 50033, *Vogue* (E) 137
In The Evening	Same as above
Mama Told Me	Same as above
Louise Blues	*Elektra* 15, *Washington* 702, *Riverside* 12-644, *Jazz Society* 50034, *Vogue* (E) 165
Chain The Lock On My Door	Same as above
Baby Baby Blues	—
Custard Pie	—
Kansas City	—
Old Woman Blues	—
Little Annie-1	*Elektra* 15, *Jazz Society* 50034, *Vogue* (E) 165
Down In The Bottom Blues-1	Same as above
Late One Saturday Evening (Night)-1	—
Hard Luck Blues-1	—

SONNY (HOOTIN') TERRY AND HIS NIGHT OWLS

Sonny Terry, vcl/hca; Jack Dupree, pno; Brownie McGhee, gtr; Sticks McGhee, gtr; Willie Jones, dms.

Harmonica Hop	Red Robin 110
Doggin' My Heart Around	—

SQUARE WALTON   New York City, 1953

Square Walton, vcl/gtr; Sonny Terry, hca; pno; gtr; dms.

Bad Hangover	Victor 20-5584; *Historical* 32
Gimme Your Bank Roll	Victor 20-5493; *Flyright* (E) 4705; *Highway 51* (E) 104
Fish Tail Blues	Victor 20-5584
Pepper Head Woman	Victor 20-5493; *Flyright* (E) 4705; *Highway 51* (E) 104

RALPH WILLIS   New York City, 15 January 1953

Ralph Willis, vcl/gtr; Sonny Terry, hca; Brownie McGhee, gtr; Gary Mapp, bs.

Gonna Hop On Down The Line	King 4631; *King* 1098; *Carnival* (E) 2941, 201
Do Right	King 4611; *King* 1098; *Carnival* (E) 2941, 201
Door Bell Blues	King 4631; *King* 875, 1098; *Carnival* (E) 2941, 201
Why'd You Do It	King 4611; *King* 1098; *Carnival* (E) 2941, 201

SONNY TERRY   **New York City, 27 August 1953**

Sonny Terry, vcl/hca; Fletcher Smith, pno; Mickey Baker, gtr;
Johnny Williams, bs; Marty Wilson, dms; Bobby Donaldson, bongos.

Hootin' And Jumpin'	Victor 20-5492
Sonny Is Drowsing	Victor 20-5577
I'm Gonna Rock My Wig	Victor 20-5577
Hooray, Hooray	Victor 20-5492

BROWNIE McGHEE   **New York City, 1954**

Brownie McGhee, vcl/gtr; Sonny Terry, hca; bs; dms.

Bottom Blues	Savoy 844; *Savoy* 14019; *Sharp* 2003; *Musidisc* (Fr) 956
Tell Me Baby	Savoy 872; LPs same as above
Sittin' Pretty	LPs same as above
Gone, Baby, Gone	Savoy 844; LPs same as above

Brownie McGhee, vcl/gtr; Sticks McGhee, gtr; dms.

Diamond Ring	Savoy 835; LPs same as above
So Much Trouble	Same as above
Dissatisfied Blues	LPs same as above
The Way I Feel	Same as above

SONNY TERRY   **New York City, 1 February 1954**

Sonny Terry, vcl/hca; Teddy Charles, vibes; Brownie McGhee, gtr;
Lee Stanfield, bs; Marty Wilson, dms.

Lost Jawbone	Groove 0015
Louise	—
I Took You In Baby	Unissued
Juice Head Woman	—

BROTHER JOHN SELLERS   **New York City, 10 March 1954**

Brother John Sellers, vcl; Sonny Terry, hca; Johnny Johns, gtr.

Jack Of Diamonds	*Vanguard* 7022, 9036; *Vanguard* (E) 12017; *Fontana* (E) 6005
I Love You Baby	Same as above
Let Us Run	—
I've Been Lonesome, I've Been Worried	—
Sally Go Round The Sunshine	—
Every Day I Have The Blues	—
Nobody Knows The Trouble I've Seen	—
Great Day	—
Lonesome Road	—
When I've Been Drinking	—

BILLY BLAND   **New York City, 1955**

Billy Bland, vcl; Sonny Terry, hca; pno; gtrs; dms.

Chicken Hop	Old Town 1022; Tip Top 708

BROWNIE McGHEE   **New York City, 1955**

Brownie McGhee, Vcl-1/gtr-2; Sonny Terry, vcl-3/hca-4; Coyal
McMahan, vcl-5/maraccas-6.

The Midnight Special-1, 2, 3, 4, 5, 6	*Folkways* FP 28, FA 2028,
Pick A Bale Of Cotton-1, 2, 3, 4, 5, 6	*Folkways* FP 28, FA 2028 Verve 9010
I Shall Not Be Moved-1, 2, 3, 4, 5, 6	*Folkways* FP 28, FA 2028
Raise A Ruckus Tonight (Raise The Roof)	Same as above
Mamma Blues No. 2-1, 2, 3, 4, 6	*Folkways* FP 28, FA 2028, Verve 9010
A Man Is Nothing But A Fool,-2, 3, 4, 6	*Folkways* FP 28, FA 2028
Rising Sun-2, 3, 4	*Folkways* FP 28, FA 2028, Verve 9010
In His Care-2,4,5	Same as above
Preachin'-2, 4, 5	Same as above

        New York City, October, 1955

Brownie McGhee, vcl/gtr; Sonny Terry, hca; Ernest Hayes, pno;
Mickey Baker, lead gtr; Leonard Gaskin, bs; Gene Brooks, dms.

When It's Love Time	Savoy 1185; *Savoy* 14019;
I'd Love To Love You	Savoy 1177; LPs same as above
Love's A Disease	Savoy 1185; *Savoy* 14019; Savoy 1185; *Savoy* 14019; *Sharp* 2003; *Musidisc* (Fr) 956
My Fault No. 2 (My Fault)	Savoy 1185; *Savoy* 14019; *Sharp* 2003; *Musidisc* (Fr) 956
Anna Mae	Savoy 1177

SONNY TERRY   **New York City, 7 November 1955**

Sonny Terry, vcl/hca; Brownie McGhee, Sticks McGhee, gtrs; Milt
Hinton, bs; Gene Brooks, dms.

Hootin' Blues No. 2	Groove 0135
Throw This Old Dog A Bone	Unissued
Ride and Roll	Groove 0135
Tell Me Why	Unissued

ALONZO SCALES   **New York City, 30 December 1955**

Alonzo Scales, vcl; Sonny Terry, hca; pno; gtr; bs; dms.

Hard Luck Child	Wing 90049; *Flyright* (E) 4705
We Just Can't Agree	Same as above

SONNY TERRY   **New York City, 1956**

Sonny Terry, vcl/hca; pno; gtr; bs; dms.

Fast Freight Blues	Josie 828
Dangerous Woman	—

Sonny Terry, vcl/hca; Bob Gaddy, pno; Brownie McGhee, gtr.

Uncle Bud	Old Town 1023
Climbing On Top Of The Hill	Old Town 1023

BLIND GARY DAVIS   **April, 1956**

Blind Gary Davis, vcl/gtr; Sonny Terry, vcl-2/hca-1.

Death Is Riding Every Day-1	*Stinson* 56
Jesus Met The Woman At The Well-1	—
Oh, What A Beautiful City-1	—
Say No To The Devil-1	—
Motherless Children-1, 2	—
Bad Company Brought Me Here-1	—
I Can't Make The Journey By Myself-1	—
You Got To Move-1	—

SONNY TERRY   **San Francisco, 15 March 1957**

Sonny Terry, vcl/hca; Brownie McGhee, vcl/gtr.

I Got Fooled	*Fantasy* 3254
No Need Of Running	—
I Feel So Good	—
Thinkin' And Worryin'	—
I Love You Baby	—
California Blues	—
Walkin' And Lyin' Blues	—
First And Last Love	—
Christine	—
I Have Had My Fun	—
Whoopin' And Squallin'	—
Water Boy Cry	—
Motherless Child	—
Sportin' Life	—

BIG BILL BROONZY   **Chicago, 7 May 1957**

Big Bill Broonzy, vcl/gtr(-1); Sonny Terry, vcl/hca(-2); Brownie
McGhee, vcl/gtr(-3)

Keys To The Highway-1, 2, 3	*Folkways* FS 3817
Crow Jane-2	—
Louise-2	*Xtra* (E) 1004
Blues-1, 2, 3	
Beautiful City-2	—
When The Saints Go Marching In-1, 2, 3	—

BROWNIE McGHEE **New York City, November, 1957**

Brownie McGhee, vcl-2/gtr; Sonny Terry, vcl-1/hca; Gene Moore, dms.

Better Day-1, 2	*Folkways* 2327, 31024; *Verve/Folkways* 9019
Confusion-1, 2	Same as above
Dark Road-1, 2	—
John Henry-1, 2	—
Let Me Make A Little Money-1, 2	—
Old Jabo-1	—
If You Lose Your Money-1, 2	—
Guitar Highway-2	—
Heart in Sorrow-1, 2	—
Preachin' The Blues-1, 2	—
Can't Help Myself-2	—
I Love You Baby-1	—
Best Of Friends-1	—

SONNY TERRY **New York City, 1958**

Sonny Terry, vcl-1/hca-2; Sticks McGhee, vcl-3/gtr-4; J. C. Burris, hca-5, bones-6, hand slapping-7, unk. bs dm-8.

My Baby Leaving-1, 2, 4, 5	*Folkways* FA 2369
You Keep On Dogging Me-2, 3, 4, 5	—
Jail House Blues-2, 3, 4, 5	—
I've Been A Long, Long, Way-2, 3, 4, 5	—
Easy Rider-1, 2, 4, 5	—
Harmonica Jump-2, 5, 8	—
Pete's Jump-1, 2, 4, 5	—
Drink Of Wine, Mop Mop-1, 2 3, 4, 5	—
My Baby Gone Home-2, 3, 4, 5	—
Blues All Around My Bed-1, 2, 5, 8	—
Poor Man But A Good Man-1, 2 3, 6, 8	—
Harmonica With Slaps-2, 7, 8	—

BROWNIE McGHEE AND **London, 2 May 1958**
SONNY TERRY

Brownie McGhee, vcl-1/gtr; Sonny Terry, vcl-2/hca; Pat Halcox, tpt-3; Chris Barber, tbn-4; Monty Sunshine, cl-5; Eddie Smith, bj-6; Dick Smith, bs-7; Graham Burbidge, dms-8.

This Little Light Of Mine-2, 8	*Nixa* (E) 515; *Metronome* (E) 1706
Glory 2-8	*Nixa* (E) 515, 1073; *Metronome* (E) 1706, 1352
Custard Pie-2, 5, 6	*Nixa* (E) 515, 1073
Key To The Highway-1, 6	*Nixa* (E) 515, 1073; *Metronome* (E) 1706

BROWNIE McGHEE **London, 7 May 1958**

Brownie McGhee, vcl-1/gtr-2/pno-3; Sonny Terry, vcl/hca; Dave Lee, pno-4.

Black Horse Blues-3, 4	*Nixa* (E) 1060
Sonny's Blues-4	*Nixa* (E) 18; *World Record Club* (E) 379; *Roulette* 25074
Treated Wrong-1, 2	Same as above
	London, 8 May 1958
Change The Lock-2	*Nixa* (E) 18; *World Record Club* (E) 379; *Roulette* 25074
You'd Better Mind-1, 3	*Nixa* (E) 18, 1074; *World Record* *Club* (E) 379; *Roulette* 25074
Corn Bread, Peas And Black Molasses-1, 2, 4	Same as above
I Love You Baby-2, 4	—
Climbing On Top Of The Hill-1, 2	—

Newport, R.I., 11/12 July 1959

Brownie McGhee, vcl/gtr; Sonny Terry, vcl/hca.

Pick A Bale Of Cotton	*Vanguard* 9063, 2054; *Top Rank* (E) 35/071
My Baby Done Changed The Lock On The Door	Same as above
Midnight Special	*Folkways* 2432
Living With The Blues	—

BROWNIE McGHEE &
SONNY TERRY **New York City, 1959**

Brownie McGhee, vcl/gtr; Sonny Terry, hca; Bob Gaddy, pno; bs; dms;

She Loves So Easy	Old Town 1075
I Need A Woman	Same as above

Brownie McGhee, vcl/gtr; Sonny Terry, vcl-1/hca.

Oh Lawdy Pick A Bale Of Cotton-1	Choice 1; *Choice* 100, 500; *Sound* *Of America* 2001; *Top Rank* (Sw) 150
The Ballad Of John Henry	Choice 1; *Choice* 100, 500; *Sound* *Of America* 2001; *Top Rank* (E) 1007
Take This Hammer Whup	*Choice* 100, 500; *Sound Of* *America* 2001
On The Rock Island Line-1	*Choice* 100, 500; *Sound Of* *America* 2001; *Top Rank* (Sw) 150
Go And I Will Send Thee	*Choice* 100, 500; *Sound Of* *America* 2001
I'm Gonna Tell God	*Choice* 100, 500; *Sound Of* *America* 2001; *Top Rank* (E) 1007
Skip To My Lou	*Choice* 100, 500; *Sound Of* *America* 2001; *Top Rank* (Sw) 150; *Top Rank* (E) 1007
Little Sally Walker	*Choice* 100, 500; *Sound Of* *America* 2001; *Top Rank* (E) 1007
Cindy, Cindy	*Choice* 100, 500; *Sound Of* *America* 2001; *Top Rank* (Sw) 150; *Top Rank* (E) 1007
Old McDonald	*Choice* 100, 500; *Sound Of* *America* 2001
King William	Same as above
Around The Crab Apple Tree	—
In And Out The Window	—
My Mommy Told Me	—

London, 7 October 1959

Brownie McGhee, vcl-1/gtr; Sonny Terry, vcl-2/hca, Dave Lee, pno-3.

Rockin' And Whoopin'-2, 3	*Columbia* (E) 4433, 8226 33SX 1223; *Verve* 3008
Talking Harmonica Blues-2	Same as above
I Was Born With The Blues-1, 3	*Columbia* (E) 33SX1223; *Metro-* *nome* (E) 1456; *Verve* 3008
Jet Plane Blues-2	*Columbia* (E) 33SX1223; *Verve* 3008
Hound Dog Holler-2	Same as above
Fighting A Losing Battle-1, 2, 3	—
Crazy Man Blues-2, 3	—
Doctor Brownie's Famous Cure 1, 3	*Columbia* (E) 33SX1223; *Verve* 3008; *Metronome* (E) 1457
Sonny's Easy Rider-1, 2, 3	*Columbia* (E) 33SX1223; *Verve* 3008
Walk On-1, 3	*Columbia* (E) 33SX1223; *Verve* 3008; *Metronome* (E) 1456

Los Angeles, 29 December 1959

Brownie McGhee, vcl-1/gtr; Sonny Terry, vcl-2/hca.

Key To The Highway-1	*World Pacific* 1294; *Fontana* (E) 688 006; *Vogue* (E) 12247, 5014; *Minit* (E) 40005
Lose Your Money-1, 2	Same as above
Louise-2	—
Sporting Life-1	—
New Harmonica Breakdown	*World Pacific* 1294; *Fontana* (E) 688 006; *Vogue* (E) 12247, 5014
Prison Bound-1	Same as above
Livin' With The Blues-1	*World Pacific* 1294, 20150; *Fontana* (E) 688 006; *Vogue* (E) 12247, 5014
Blowing The Fuses	*World Pacific* 1294; *Fontana* (E) 688 006; *Vogue* (E) 12247, 5014
Baby Please Don't Go-1, 2	*World Pacific* 1294, 20150; *Fontana* (E) 688 006; *Vogue* (E) 12247, 5014
Twelve Gates To The City-2	*World Pacific* 1294; *Fontana* (E) 688 006; *Vogue* (E) 12247, 5014
Pawnshop Blues-1	Same as above
Brownie's Guitar Blues	—

	New York City, 1960
Pawn Shop-1	Bluesville 809; *Bluesville* 1002; *Prestige* 14013
Let Me Be Your Big Dog-1	*Bluesville* 1002; *Prestige* 14013; *Metronome* (E) 9021; *Bluesville* 802
You Don't Know-1	*Bluesville* 1002; *Prestige* 14013
Betty And Dupree Blues-1	Same as above
Back To New Orleans-2	Same as above
Stranger Here-1, 2	Bluesville 1002; *Bluesville* 1002; *Prestige* 14013
Fox Hunt-1	*Bluesville* 1002; *Prestige* 14013
I'm Prison Bound-1	*Bluesville* 1002; *Prestige* 14013; *Metronome* (E) 9021
Louise, Louise-1	Same as above
Baby, How Long-1	—
Freight Train-1	*Bluesville* 1002; *Prestige* 14013
Too Nicey Mama-1, 2	Bluesville 809; *Bluesville* 1005
Sonny's Squall-1	*Bluesville* 1005
Red River Blues-1, 2	—
Gone Gal-1	—
Blues Before Sunrise-1	—
Sweet Lovin' Kind-1, 2	—
Midnight Special-1, 2	—
Take This Hammer Whup-1, 2	—
Meet Me Down The Bottom-1	—
Tryin' To Win-1, 2	—
Beggin' And Cryin'	Bluesville 818; *Bluesville* 1020
My Plan	*Bluesville* 1020
Trying To Destroy Me	—
Everything I Had Is Gone	—
Jealous Man	—
Understand Me	—
Blues Of Happiness	—
Blues All Round My Head-2	*Bluesville* 1020; *Prestige* 7715
East Coast Blues-1	Same as above
Muddy Water-1	—

SONNY TERRY   New York City, 1960

Sonny Terry, vcl/hca; J. C. Burris, hca-1; Sticks McGhee, gtr; Belton Evans, dms-2.

I Ain't Gonna Be Your Dog No More	*Bluesville* 1025; *Xtra* (E) 5025
My Baby Done Gone-1, 2	Same as above
Worried Blues	—
High Powered Woman-1	—
Pepperheaded Woman-1	—
Sonny's Story-1	—
I'm Gonna Get On My Feet Afterwhile-1, 2	—
Four O'Clock Blues-1, 2	—
Telephone Blues-1, 2	—
Great Tall Engine-1, 2	—

STICKS McGHEE

Sticks McGhee, vcl/gtr; Sonny Terry, hca; J. C. Burris, gtr; dms.

Money Fever	Herald 553; *Flyright* (E) 4706
Sleep In Job	— —

BROWNIE McGHEE

Brownie McGhee, vcl-1/gtr; Sonny Terry, vcl-2/hca.

Walk On-1, 2	Vee Jay 1138; *Archive of Folk Music* 242; *Olympic* 7108; *Verve Folkways* 3011; *Horizon* (E) 1617; *Joy* (E) 175
Blues For The Lowlands-1	Same as above
Down By The Riverside-1	Vee Jay 1138; *Archive of Folk Music* 242; *Olympic* 7108; Horizon *Horizon* (E) 1617; *Joy* (E) 175
Blowin' The Fuses	Vee Jay 1138; *Archive of Folk Music* 242; *Olympic* 7108; *Joy* (E) 175
Just Rode In Your Town-1, 2	*Archive of Folk Music* 242; *Olympic* 7108; *Verve/Folkways* 3011; *Society* (E) 105
Sun's Gonna Shine-1	*Verve/Folkways* 3011; *Olympic* 7108; *Society* (E) 1015
Po' Boy-2	*Verve/Folkways* 3012; *Olympic* 7108; *Society* (E) 1015
Drinking The Blues-2	Same as above

Sonny Terry, vcl-1/hca; Brownie McGhee, vcl/gtr.

I'm A Stranger Here-1	*Archive of Folk Music* 242
Trouble In Mind	—

Brownie McGhee, vcl-1/gtr; Sonny Terry, vcl-2/hca; Roy Haynes, dms.

I Got A Woman-1, 2	*Bluesville* 1033; *Prestige* 7715
Don't You Lie To Me-1	Same as above
Hold Me In Your Arms-1	*Bluesville* 1033
The C.C. and O. Blues-1	—
That's Why I'm Walking-1, 2	—
Wrong Track-1	—
Blue Feeling-1	—
House Lady-1	—
I Know Better-1	—
The Devil's Gonna Get You-1	—

LIGHTNIN' HOPKINS   Los Angeles, 6 July 1960

Lightnin' Hopkins, vcl/gtr; Brownie McGhee, vcl-1/gtr-2; Sonny Terry, vcl-3/hca-4; Big Joe Williams, vcl-5/gtr-6; Jimmy Bonds, bs-7.

Ain't Nothin' Like Whisky 1-7	*World Pacific* 1296, 1817, 20150; *Kimberly* 2017
If You Steal My Chickens You Can't Make 'Em Lay 1-7	Same as above
Penitentiary Blues 1-7	*World Pacific* 1296, 1817, 20150
Wimmen From Coast To Coast 1-7	*World Pacific* 1296, 1817; *Kimberly* 2017
Chain Gang Blues-1, 2, 4, 5, 6, 7	*World Pacific* 1296; *Verve/Folkways* 3012
New Car Blues (Brand New Car) 2, 3, 4, 5, 6, 7 (No Hopkins vcl)	*Society* (E) 1015; 1020; *Archive of Folk Music* 241; *Verve/Folkways* 3012
You Gonna Need Somebody To Go Your Bond (I've Been Scorned)-1-7	*Society* (E) 1020; *Verve/Folkways* 3012; *Archive Of Folk Music* 241
Three Aces On The Bottom Of The Deal (Blues For Gamblers) 1, 2, 3, 4	*Vee Jay* 1138; *Horizon* (E) 1617; *Joy* (E) 175; *Society* (E) 1009, 1020; *Archive Of Folk Music* 242
I'm Gonna Mourn On That Shore (Right On That Shore)-1, 2, 3, 4	Same as above + *Olympic* 7108
Four Friends Blues (Unk. acc.)	Unissued
Friends And Pals (Unk. acc.)	—
Blues From The Bottom (Unk. Acc.)	—

	New Jersey, October, 1960

Lightnin' Hopkins, vcl/gtr; Sonny Terry, vcl-1/hca-2.

Got To Move Your Baby-2	Bluesville 813; *Bluesville* 101, 1029, 1081; *Prestige* 7831, 7592
So Sorry To Leave You-2	*Bluesville* 101, 1029, 1081; *Prestige* 7831
Last Night Blues-2	Bluesville 821; *Bluesville* 101, 1029, 1081; *Prestige* 7592, 7831
Lightnin's Stroke-2	*Bluesville* 101; 1029, 1081; *Prestige* 7831
Hard To Love A Woman-2	Bluesville 817; *Bluesville* 101, 1029, 1081; 1084; *Prestige* 7592, 7831
Conversation Blues-1, 2	Bluesville 817; *Bluesville* 1029, 1081, 101; *Prestige* 7831

SONNY TERRY   New York City, October, 1960

Sonny Terry, vcl/hca; Lightnin' Hopkins, gtr-1; Brownie McGhee, gtr-2; Leonard Gaskin, bs-3; Belton Evans, dms-4.

One Monkey Don't Stop The Show-1, 3, 4	*Prestige* 7802; *Bluesville* 1059
Changed The Lock On The Door-1, 3, 4	— —
Tater Pie-1, 3, 4	— —
She's So Sweet-1, 3, 4	— —
Diggin' My Potatoes-1, 3, 4	— —
Sonny's Comin'-2 (no vcl)	—
Ida Mae-2	— —
Callin' My Mama-2 (no vcl)	— —
Bad Luck-2	— —
Blues From The Bottom-2	— —

	New York City, 1961

Sonny Terry, vcl-1/hca-2/jawharp-3; Brownie McGhee, vcl-4/gtr-5; J. C. Burris, bones-6/hca-7.

Shortnin' Bread-3, 5	*Folkways* 3821
Beautiful City-1, 3, 5, 6	—

Whoop And Holler-1, 2, 5, 6	—
My Baby's Gone-1, 2, 5, 6	—
Dirty Mistreater-1, 2, 5, 7	—
Pick A Bale Of Cotton-3, 5, 6	—
I've Been Your Doggie Since I've Been Your Man-1, 2, 5, 6	—
Skip To My Lou-3, 5, 6	—
Crow Jane-1, 2, 5, 6	—
Blues From Everywhere-2, 4, 5, 7	—
Fox Chase-2, 3, 5, 6	—
Harmonica Blues-2, 5, 6	—
Bottle Up And Go-1, 2, 5, 7	—

SONNY TERRY, BROWNIE McGHEE & CASEY HART   **New York City, 1961**

Sonny Terry, hca; Brownie McGhee, vcl-1/gtr-2/whistling-3; Casey Hart, vcl-4; Lord Westbrook, gtr-5; Leonard Gaskin, bs-6; Robert Banks, org-7; Bobby Donaldson, dms-8.

Hootin'-5, 6, 8	Choice 15; *Choice* 503
Dupre'-5, 6, 8	Same as above
Country Road (Old Town Blues)	*Choice* 503
Right Now-1, 2	—
The Rider-5, 6, 7	—
If You Don't Want Me-4, 5, 6, 7, 8	—
What More You Want Me To Do-4, 5, 6, 7, 8	—
Trying To Forget-4, 5, 6, 7, 8	—
Call Today-4, 5, 6, 7, 8	Choice 14; *Choice* 503
Blues For My Baby-4, 5, 6, 7, 8	Same as above

SONNY TERRY & BROWNIE McGHEE

Sonny Terry, hca; Brownie McGhee, vcl/gtr.

You Hear Me Talkin'	*Choice* 509
I'm Goin Down Slow	—
Raise A Rukas Tonight	—
C. C. Rider	—
Careless Love	—
Worried Life Blues	—
Crawdad Hole	—
Jelly Roll	—
Ain't Gonna Study War	—
Key To The Highway	—

LUKE 'LONG GONE' MILES   **Los Angeles, 1961**

Luke Miles, vcl; Sonny Terry, hca; Brownie McGhee, gtr.

Long Gone	Smash 1755
War Time Blues	—

SONNY TERRY   **San Francisco, early 1961**

Sonny Terry, vcl/hca; Brownie McGhee, vcl/gtr.

You Can't Hide	Fantasy 546; *Fantasy* 3296
I Shall Not Be Moved	—; *Vocalion* (E) 1279
Just A Closer Walk	*Fantasy* 3296
Children Go Where I Send Thee	—
What A Beautiful City	—
Glory, Glory	—
If I Could Hear My Mother Pray	—
I'm Going To Shout	—
Packing Up	—; *Vocalion* (E) 1279
Get Right Church	—
Some Of These Days	—
If You See My Saviour	— —; *Vocalion* (E) 1279
John Henry	*Fantasy* 3317
Cornbread And Peas	—
Louise	—
I Done Done	—
Meet You In The Morning	—
Poor Boy From Home	—
Hudy Leadbelly	—
Something's Wrong At Home	—
Take This Hammer	—
Baby's Gone	—
Lose Your Money	—
I'm A Stranger	—

San Francisco, December, 1961

Sonny Terry, vcl-1/hca; Brownie McGhee, vcl-2/gtr.

Hooray, Hooray, This Woman Is Killing Me-1	*Fantasy* 3340, 8091
Born To Live The Blues-2	— —
Just About Crazy-1	— —
Up, Sometimes Down-2	— —
Baby, I knocked On Your Door-1	— —
Keep On Walking-1, 2	— —
Baby, I Got My Eye On You-1, 2	— —
I Got A Little Girl-1	— —
I Feel Alright Now-2	— —
Worry, Worry, Worry-2	— —
Sweet Woman Blues-1	— —

BROWNIE McGHEE   **New York City, 1962**

Brownie McGhee, vcl/gtr; Sonny Terry, hca; Bennie Foster, gtr.

Jump Little Children	*Prestige* 7715; *Prestige/ Bluesville* 1042
Little Black Engine	Same as above
Lonesome Day	*Prestige/Bluesville* 1042
One Thing For Sure	—
The Killin' Floor	—
I Don't Know The Reason	—
Trouble In Mind	—
Everyday I Have The Blues	—
Door To Success	—

SONNY TERRY & BROWNIE McGHEE   **Philadelphia, April 1962**

Sonny Terry, vcl-1/hca; Brownie McGhee, vcl-2/gtr.

Evil Hearted Me-2	*Prestige* 7803; *Prestige/ Bluesville* 1058
Sick Man-1	Same as above
Barking Bull Dog-2	—
Spread The News Around-1, 2	—
Backwater Blues-2	—
Custard Pie-1, 2	—
Wholesale Dealin' Papa-2	—
Motocycle Blues-1	—
Hand In Hand-2	—
I Woke Up One Morning And I Could Hardly See-1	—

SONNY TERRY   **Hamburg, Germany, 18 Oct. 1962**

Sonny Terry, vcl/hca; Brownie McGhee, gtr; T-Bone Walker, pno; Willie Dixon, bs.

I'm Crazy 'Bout You Baby	*Polydor Special* (E) 236 216

BROWNIE McGHEE   **Newport, R.I., 1963**

Brownie McGhee, vcl-1/gtr; Sonny Terry, vcl-2/hca.

Long Gone-2	*Vanguard* 9145, 79145
Walk On-1	Same as above
Key To The Highway-1	*Vanguard* 9145, 79145, 25/26

SONNY TERRY & BROWNIE McGHEE   **Chicago, 1967?**

Sonny Terry, vcl-1/hca; Brownie McGhee, vcl-2/gtr.

Ride and Roll-1, 2	*Fontana* 67599
Love, Truth & Confidence-1	—
Ida B-1	—
Baby, I Got My Mind Off You-1	—
I'll Be Anything-2	—
Don't Pity Me-2	—
Whoee, Whoee-1	—
I Gotta Look Under Your Hood-2	—
C'Mon If You're Comin'-2	—
Burnt Child Afraid Of Fire-1, 2	—
Amen-2	—

Los Angeles, 1 March 1969

Sonny Terry, vcl-1/hca; Brownie McGhee, vcl-2/gtr; Ray Johnson, pno-3/elect. pno-4/tamburine-5; Jimmy Bond, bs; Panama Francis, dms.

123

Long Way From Home-1, 3	*Bluesway* 6028
Big Question-2, 4	—
Rock Island Line-1, 2, 5	—
Night and Day-1, 3	—
You Just Usin' Me For A Convenience-2, 3	—
Hole In The Wall-1, 2, 3	—
Life Is A Gamble-2, 4	—
Don't Mistreat Me-1, 3	—
Packin' Up, Gettin' Ready-1, 2, 3, 5	—
Wailin' And Whoopin'-4, 5	—
B. M. Special-3, 5	—

Los Angeles, 24 September 1969

Sonny Terry, vcl-1/hca; Brownie McGhee, vcl-2/gtr; Earl Hooker, gtr; Ray Johnson, pno-3/elect. pno-4; Jimmy Bond, bs; Panama Francis, dms; Vocal trio-5

Black Cat Bone-1, 2, 3	*Bluesway* 6059
Brownie's New Blues-2, 4	—
Poor Man Blues-1, 4	—
Tell Me Why-2, 3	—
My Baby's So Fine-1, 3	—
Don't Wait For Me-2, 3, 5	—
I'm In Love With You Baby-1, 4	—
Parcel Post Blues-2, 3	—
When I Was Drinkin'-1, 4	—
I Couldn't Believe My Eyes-2, 3	—

Frankfort, Germany, 16 Nov. 1970

Sonny Terry, vcl-1/hca; Brownie McGhee, vcl-2/gtr; Jack Dupree, pno-3; Willie Dixon, bs-4; Clifton James, dms-5.

Hootin' The Blues-1	*Scout* (G) 7
Walk On-1, 2, 3, 4, 5	—

SONNY TERRY Copenhagen, 13 November 1971

Sonny Terry, vcl/hca; Brownie McGhee, gtr-1; Leif Johansson, wbd-2; Svend Erik Norregard, dms-3.

Digging My Potatoes-1, 2	*Storyville* (D) 218
Freight Train Rollin' On-1, 2	—
Old Lost John	—
Cousin John	—
Take This Hammer-1	—
I'm Afraid Of Fire-1	—
The Harmonica Blues-2	—
Goin' Down Slow-2	—
Easy Rider-1, 3	—
I'm Crazy About Your Pie-1, 3	—

Copenhagen, 14 November 1971

Sonny Terry, vcl/hca; Brownie McGhee, gtr-1.

Chasing The Fox	*Storyville* (D) 218
Pretty Little Girl-1	—

SONNY TERRY & Hollywood, Cal., 1972
BROWNIE McGHEE

Brownie McGhee, vcl-1/gtr-2; Sonny Terry, vcl-3/hca; Arlo Guthrie, vcl-4/gtr-5/pno-6; Michael Franks, gtr-7/bjo-8; Harry Holt, bs-9; Maurice Rogers, pno-10/elect pno-11/thumb piano-12/moog-13; Sugarcane Harris, vln-14; Al McKay, gtr-15; Jerry McGhee, gtr-16/dobro-17; Eddie Greene, dms-18; John Mayall, vcl-19/hca-20/elect 12 string gtr-21/pno-27; Jerry Cole, gtr-22/bjo-23/dobro-24; John Hammond, gtr-25; vcl trio-26.

People Get Ready-1, 2, 5, 7, 9, 11, 15, 18, 26	*A&M* 4379
Bring It On Home To Me-1, 2, 3, 9, 10, 14, 17, 18	—
You Bring Out The Boogie In Me-1, 2, 7, 9, 10, 16, 18	—
Sail Away-1, 3, 4, 5, 8, 9, 10, 12, 18, 22, 26	—
Sonny's Thing-2, 14, 18, 19, 21	—
The Battle Is Over (But The War Goes On) 1, 2, 9, 10, 11, 15, 16, 18, 21	—
Walkin' My Blues Away-1, 2, 3, 9, 16, 18, 27, 22, 25	—
Jesus Gonna Make It Alright-1, 2, 9, 10, 17, 18, 26	—
God And Man-1, 2, 3, 6, 7, 18, 24, 26	—
On The Road Again-1, 2, 3, 7, 9, 11, 15, 18	—
Big Wind (Is A Comin')-1, 2, 7, 9, 13, 18, 23, 26	*Impress* 717; *A&M* 4379
White Boy Lost In The Blues 1, 2, 3, 9, 11, 18, 19, 20, 27	*A&M* 4379
White Boy Lost In The Blues 1, 2, 3, 9, 11, 18, 20	*Impress* 717

SONNY TERRY New York City, 25 April 1974

Sonny Terry, vcl-1/hca-2; Bob Malenky, vcl-3/gtr-4; Michael Rura, pno-5.

Feel Like Robbin' The Grave 1, 2, 3, 4, 5	*Blue Labor* 101
Selling Out-1, 2, 4, 5	—
Black Night Road-2, 3, 4	—
That Train And My Woman-1, 2, 4, 5	—
Playing With The Thing-2, 5	—
Cut Off From My Baby-1, 2, 4, 5	—
Mean Old Woman-1, 2, 5	—
One Woman Man-2, 3, 4	—
Cold Wind Blowing-1, 2, 4, 5	—
The Boogie-5	—

Record Permissions

Lost John/Sonny Terry
From the album "Sonny Terry," The Everest Archive of Folk Music.
Used by Permission.

Harmonica With Slaps/Sonny Terry and J. C. Burris
From Folkways Records FA 2369. Used by Permission of Moses Asch.

I Got My Eyes On You/Sonny Terry
From Fantasy 8091.
Used by Permission, Fantasy Record Co., Berkeley, Ca. 94710

Baby, I Knocked On Your Door/Sonny Terry
From Fantasy 8091.
Used by Permission, Fantasy Record Co., Berkeley, Ca. 94710

My Baby Leaving/Sonny Terry
From Folkways Records FA 2369. Used by permission of Moses Asch.

Poor Man But A Good Man/Sonny Terry and J. C. Burris
From Folkways Records FA 2369. Used by permission of Moses Asch.

Keep On Walking/Brownie McGhee
From Fantasy 8091.
Used by Permission, Fantasy Record Co., Berkeley, Ca. 94710

Sweet Woman Blues/Sonny Terry
From Fantasy 8091.
Used by Permission, Fantasy Record Co., Berkeley, Ca. 94107

Easy Rider/Adapted by Sonny Terry
From Folkways Records FA 2369. Used by permission of Moses Asch.

Blues All Around My Bed/Adapted by Sonny Terry and J. C. Burris
From Folkways Records FA 2369. Used by permission of Moses Asch.

Mean Old Woman/Sonny Terry and Emma Terry
From Sonny Terry's "Robbin' The Grave" BL 101.
BLUE LABOR Records, 106 Haven Avenue New York, N.Y. 10032. (212) 228-5632.

I Got A Little Girl/Sonny Terry
From Fantasy 8091.
Used by Permission, Fantasy Record Co., Berkeley, Ca. 94710

Cold Wind Blowin'/Bob Malenky and Kent Cooper
From Sonny Terry's "Robbin' The Grave" BL 101.
BLUE LABOR Records, 106 Haven Avenue, New York, N.Y. 10032. (212) 228-5632.

Two Outstanding Blues Harp Books
by Tony Glover

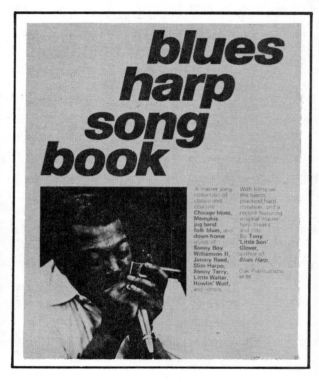

Blues Harp

by Tony "Harp Dog" Glover

Here is a hearty, entertaining and irreverent survey of the blues, R&B and the origins of rock, incorporated in a very complete instruction manual for playing harmonica, blues style. Based on the playing of such giants as Sonny Boy Williamson, Little Walter, Jimmy Reed and Sonny Terry, *Blues Harp* covers basic and advanced techniques, as well as how to choose your ax, how harps work and how to work them, solo or lead harp vs. accompanying, guitar/harp relationships, amplified harp, and instruction on the care of the instrument. In his earthy, witty style, Tony Glover also discusses the history and people connected with the harp and gives advice on some common sense practices for the harp player. There's even a section dealing with old-time tips, such as how to produce amusing sound effects by playing the harp through your ear, under glass, through a hose or while dancing. This book comes complete with two records, a bibliography, discography and index, and is fully illustrated with photos of the artists and instructional diagrams.

Oak Publications/$4.95

Order no: 000018

Blues Harp Songbook

by Tony "Harp Dog" Glover

This is a master song collection of both classic and obscure harp music, and the long-awaited follow-up to *Blues Harp*. As a special feature, it includes a seven-inch record, which is not an instructional play-along but instead presents nineteen rare and hard to get excerpts from original blues recordings by the masters of the blues harp. This book is recommended for the experienced harp player and covers almost fifty years of blues harp music. There are over twenty tunes in harp tablature, from the down-home jug band styles of Ollis Martin and Will Shade, to the country blues style of Sonny Terry and Brownie McGhee, to the Chicago blues of Junior Wells, Little Walter, Sonny Boy Williamson and Howlin' Wolf. It contains instructive notes on playing the blues harp, techniques like bending, slurring, playing electrified harp and more, a complete discography, plus biographies on each artist, and the low-key, no-holds-barred language in which it's written makes for really entertaining reading.

Oak Publications/$6.95 with recording.

Order no: 000157